A Word in Season
Vol. II

Spring — Summer

by
Dick Mills

HARRISON HOUSE
Tulsa, Oklahoma

Unless otherwise indicated, all Scripture quotations
are taken from the *King James Version* of the Bible.

A Word in Season, Vol. II
Spring — Summer
ISBN 0-89274-427-8
Copyright © 1987 by Dick Mills
P. O. Box 758
Hemet, California 92343

Published by Harrison House, Inc.
P. O. Box 35035
Tulsa, Oklahoma 74153

**And they heard the sound of the Lord God
walking in the garden in the cool of the day . . . .**
Genesis 3:8 NKJ

The cool of the day is around 4:00 p.m. It is the time
when the evening breeze begins to stir. The Hebrew word
translated **cool** in this verse is *ruwach (roo'-ach)*. Elsewhere
in Scripture, this same word is translated *breath, wind, breeze,
spirit,* and *Holy Spirit.*

God is a spirit. When the afternoon breeze began to stir
in the Garden of Eden, God as a spirit came to Adam and
Eve in the wind. Although it is not stated that this was a
daily occurrence, most Bible scholars consulted seemed to
feel that this was the case.

David Kimchi, a Jewish scholar living in Spain in the
12th century, wrote that Adam and Eve sinned around the
4:00 p.m. time. Satan's stratagem was to tempt Adam and
Eve into disobedience, thereby creating a sin barrier between
them and their God.

Matthew Henry, an 18th-century scholar, wrote: "There
is an evangelic note to this passage. God knew they had
sinned, but it did not keep Him from coming to meet them.
Even though they had miserably failed and caused a separa-
tion between God and the pair, He still came looking for
them. His grief and compassion effected a reconciliation and
a promise of a coming Messiah."

To this day, man is still feeling the effects of that separa-
tion. I believe modern man is still lonely for his Creator's
fellowship. There is a void, a darkness, in his heart. Jesus
came to fill that void. To those who believe, He has promised
the light of His eternal presence — 24 hours a day. To the
Christian, there is no such thing as a "twilight zone"!

". . . to make ready a people prepared for the Lord."
Luke 1:17 NKJ

Even though these two phrases, **make ready** and **prepared,** are seemingly synonymous, they have opposite meanings in the original Hebrew. The word translated **make ready** is used to describe thorough preparation by an internal fitness. The word rendered **prepared** refers to external equipment and adjustment. One describes a work of grace going on outside of the Christian Church, the other a work of grace going on within the Church.

Make ready in this verse covers the whole range of internal qualifications necessary to meet the Lord Jesus at His return. The Holy Spirit is working inside each believer in the areas of honesty, integrity, humility, holiness, obedience, attitude, and motive. An invisible work of grace is going on in God's people helping them to overcome resentment, bitterness, hurts, wounds, unforgiveness, and general unbelief.

Prepared is a description of the external work of grace, including the Church's coming into unity. Revival fires burning, true worshippers showing forth the praises of God, Christians standing shoulder to shoulder against the common enemy, and rallying around to help in international disasters: these are externals that are visible to the unbelieving world.

In this prophetic note, the Lord declares that an internal work is going on that will cause the Church to be externally prepared for His Second Coming. God is at work within each believer (Phil. 2:13), perfecting us and maturing us. He is also at work externally in the world at large, getting His Church ready. The Bride of Christ is becoming more beautiful every single day!

**"...the Egyptians whom you see today,
you shall see again no more forever."**
Exodus 14:13,14 NKJ

How would you like to bid a "final farewell" to your problems as you go on to your promised land? How would you like to say goodbye forever to worry, fear, and anxiety? To cancer, arthritis, diabetes, heart trouble? To poverty, debt, unemployment, and money worries? Does this sound too good to be true? Can you accept this promise from the Lord: **". . . the Egyptians whom you see today, you shall see again no more forever?"** Can you claim this promise without a qualifying "Yes, but . . ."?

In Biblical typology, Egypt is a picture of the world system and everything related to it. When we read that Israel was told not to look to Egypt for help (Is. 30:2), it is a message for us today to rely completely upon the Lord as our sole source of supply. Israel was warned of the Lord: **". . . the Egyptians shall help in vain and to no purpose"** (Is. 30:7 *NKJ*). So Egypt can be compared to dependence upon man and man's resources. Such faith is always misplaced. We Christians are urged to put our total trust in the Lord.

Biblical Egypt also represents the opposition and hostility shown to God's people, as in Moses' day. This situation can be likened to the modern-day problems we Christians face with persecution, poverty, pressure, and life's adversity.

Praise God, there is a time of deliverance. No trouble was ever intended to be permanent. The "Egyptians" you see today, you will see no more. The problems you have been facing up till now, you will never face again.

But we have this treasure in earthen vessels . . . .
2 Corinthians 4:7 NKJ

This verse presents a divine paradox: immutable deity dwelling in a breakable container...the Creator of the heavens and earth residing in a clay vessel...eternal permanence abiding in a time-captive housing.

The paradox has to do with completion and incompletion. As human beings, we are not complete till our divine Creator has taken up His abode in our hearts. For some reason known only to Him, the Almighty, the Eternal, has chosen the human heart as His place of rest. We are created with a void in our hearts which only He can fill. By His own design, neither creature nor Creator can function properly till He becomes incarnate in us. Without His Spirit, we can do nothing in our weak flesh. In His infinite wisdom He has chosen not to manifest Himself in the universe without our mortal bodies. Therefore, neither of us functions adequately without the cooperation of the other.

In the original Greek, this word translated **earthen** is *ostrakinos* which is defined as "made of clay, brittle, fragile, easily broken." God has chosen to invest His frail human creatures with a treasure of inestimable value. **Treasure** is also an interesting word. In the original Greek, it is *thesauros*. It refers to deposited wealth, amassed riches, reserves of great value, a hoard of priceless valuables.

God's Spirit in us is like all the country's gold in Fort Knox. He is the treasure, we are the vault. God has taken the riches of His Holy Spirit and stored them in our bodies. The contrast between the two is so great, He gets all the focus, the attention and the recognition!

". . . you shall be witnesses to Me . . . ."
Acts 1:8 NKJ

Jesus promised His followers an enduement of power. The end result would be their witness to the world. The Greek word translated **witnesses** here is *martus* from which we derive our English word *martyr*. We usually think of martyrs as those early Christians who were fed to the lions or burned at the stake. Church history records thousands of heroic deeds of Christian martyrs who gave their lives for the faith. Their stories have inspired many believers with new courage and strength.

Martus has other meanings in addition to martyrdom. The verb form of this word means "to testify." The Holy Spirit empowers the believer to live a life that is a testimony to others. Perhaps you are the only Christian in your office, factory or department. If so, your lifestyle should be a testimony of your Christian faith. Those around you who do not know the Lord should be able to see in your life a quality that is missing in their own. We "testify" with more than just words. How we live, how we conduct ourselves, how we react and respond in awkward and unpleasant situations is also a witness or testimony to our faith (or lack of it!). An overcoming and victorious life is a great testimony to the world.

To testify means "to give evidence or produce facts," "to exhibit truth," or "to confirm claims." One form of evidence is signs, wonders, and miracles. The early Church depended upon the Lord to confirm their witness with supernatural signs. In Acts 1:8 the Lord Jesus declared His disciples would be filled with the Holy Spirit. In Mark 16:17,18 He promised that their witness would be backed up with divine evidence.

**"You will also declare a thing, and
it will be established for you."**

Job 22:28 NKJ

The word **thing** in the original Hebrew is *omer (o'mer)* and is similar to the Greek word *rhema*. The promises, the sayings, the word, the utterance, and the confessed word are included in *omer*.

"You will also declare the Word of God, the promises of God, the sayings of God, and these things will happen." This implies more than just cheerful optimism, wishful thinking, or positive affirmation. When we speak forth the Word of God, we are not just blowing smoke, filling the air with clever rhetoric, or mouthing platitudes. We are declaring with our lips what God has spoken in our ears. The power is not in our speaking; it's in the Lord Who gives the message.

When we're in distress, people can tell us, "Don't give up; hang in there. Remember, it's always darkest before the dawn." And all that may be true and some comfort. But it really does more for us to hear the Lord say to us personally, **. . . not a hair of your head shall be lost** (Luke 21:18 NKJ). All the cute aphorisms and clever slogans in the world are anemic compared with a solid word from the Lord.

This word **declare** (or "decree") means "to decide, predetermine, and declare the outcome of a matter before it comes to pass." If your declaration is in line with the word you have received from God, you can "declare a thing, and it will be established for you!" Weak or timid faith is too cautious to make any kind of pronouncement before it sees the outcome, but strong faith says, "It shall be done just as the Lord has said!"

**I will instruct you and teach you in the way
you should go; I will guide you with My eye.**

Psalm 32:8 NKJ

This is a good verse for those of us who seek guidance and direction from the Lord. It is an assurance that our heavenly Father is going to move us from a weak transmission to a "clear-channel station with no static" so we will be able to hear the gentle voice of the Good Shepherd without interference.

The Lord makes three direct promises in this verse:

1) **I will instruct you . . .** This is like having a private tutor. The purpose of the instruction we thus receive is to make us more intelligent, skillful and circumspect in our dealings, more adept in making decisions.

2) **. . . and teach you in the way you should go; . . .** The original word used here indicates the pointing of a finger in a certain direction. It also implies shooting an arrow at a target in such a way as to avoid missing the mark. This word from the Lord is an assurance that we will not drift aimlessly through life, but that He will give us a definite direction and a clear goal to aim for.

3) **. . . I will guide you with my eye.** One translation of this phrase says: "I will keep my eye upon you to see how you are doing."

Here is my paraphrase of this verse: "I will make you skillful and proficient in decision-making and will aim you in the right direction; I will watch your progress and see how you are getting along; My eye will be upon you for your benefit."

If by any means I may provoke to emulation them which are my flesh . . . .
Romans 11:14

The English word *emulation* is only used twice in the *King James Bible* — both times by the same author, Paul. He uses the singular form in a very positive way in Romans 11:14, but the plural form in a very negative way in Galatians 5:20.

In the passage in Galatians, **emulations** (plural) is listed as one of the works of the flesh. The original Greek word used here is *zelos (dzay-los)*. When used in this context, it refers to hatred, wrath, variance, strife, jealousy or malice, the indignant zeal of an enemy. It portrays destructive energy that should be avoided at all costs.

In the passage above from Romans, **emulation** (singular) is used in a good sense. The original Greek word here is *parazeloo (par-ad-zay-lo-o)*. It refers to stimulating another person by example, or to a good-natured rivalry that brings out the best in another person. It also implies challenging or motivating a person to become more ambitious or more aggressive.

Thus, *emulation*, as used here by Paul, is a "good example." Paul is saying: "I hope my Jewish friends will see something in my life that will stir them to action to become just like me." You and I can lead lives so full of the love of God that others are inspired to become just like us. In a time when there are few heroes or positive role models, the Lord can cause us to be "exhibit A" of what Christianity is all about. Our lives should make others want what we have.

. . . and strengthen your bones . . . .
Isaiah 58:11 NKJ

This word *strengthen* has quite a few interesting definitions which can speak to us today. *Chalats (kwaw-lats')* is the original Hebrew word used by Isaiah. The King James translators rendered it "make fat" your bones. As people get older, their bones get brittle and break easily. This promise to "make fat your bones" is an assurance of plenty of moisture or marrow in the bones throughout life. Instead of our bones getting old and brittle, this word guarantees that we will remain limber and pliable all our days. For the child of God, the aging process can be reversed by this word from the Lord.

One translator reads *chalats:* "He will *arm* your bones." This translation has a military overtone. Not only are we Christians marching through life, we are traveling as soldiers to fight a war. To "arm the bones" is the same as to provide with protective armor so as to render invulnerable to attack.

Chalats is also used in the sense of stripping off excess baggage, cargo, or unnecessary weight. A person who is going on a long journey is not going to overload himself with useless and cumbersome burdens. Most wilderness backpackers learn to carry only vital provisions so they can travel light. Our God has promised to lighten our load and free us for unimpeded travel. What a wonderful word for the Lord's traveling soldiers: Plenty of moisture for the bones, arming and fortifying for battle, lightening the load so the bones can be agile and limber. It's all there to help us reach our destination and accomplish our mission.

March 10

> **"For He will finish the work and cut it short in righteousness, because the Lord will make a short work upon the earth."**
>
> **Romans 9:28** NKJ

Your God is saying to you: "Your prayer has been heard. I am intervening and responding to your petition. The answer is on its way. I am speeding up the answer, so get ready for a quick and sudden release of divine power in your situation."

The context of this verse is God's dealings with Israel, but the word expressed here can be applied to all individuals who put their trust in the Lord for answers to their prayers. When scholars attempt to confine a scripture to a certain community, society, or nation, we must remind them that such masses of people are made up of individuals. A verse spoken to a city is also a word spoken to the individual citizens of that metropolis. This is a verse for us personally, as well as a group of people.

In the Greek text of this verse, the expression **short work** is *suntemno logos. Logos* has many definitions, among them "topic," "matter," "a thing," "a report," "a subject," and "a word." *Suntemno* means "to reduce or contract the size of a thing by concise and speedy cutting." Thus we are promised here that God's Word covering final things and the consummation of time will be speeded up and shortened.

The Lord is doing a "quick work" in His Church. Do not be surprised when He accelerates: 1) your answers, 2) your growth and maturing, 3) your ability to worship Him in spirit and in truth, and 4) your desires to please Him and do His will.

. . . reaching forward to those things which are ahead.
Philippians 3:13 NKJ

Craning the neck, scanning the horizon, and shading the eyes with the hand in order to see at a distance: these are all expressed by the phrase **reaching forward.** Paul is telling the Philippians to forget the past and start looking ahead. He knew what he was talking about. Since he had earlier persecuted the Church and consented to the stoning of Stephen, Paul had to learn to put such negative memories behind him and get on with life. Instead of allowing the past to become an unbearable burden and weight to him, Paul simply dropped it to the ground and used it as a stepping stone to the future.

Reaching forward is a good exercise for all of us. It stimulates hope. It puts us in a state of expectancy. It declares that what has been is only a prologue to what will be: Yesterday was good, today is better, tomorrow will be better still. Reaching forward anticipates miracles, revivals, outpourings of the Spirit of God, deliverances, and answered prayer. It looks to the future with intensity and great expectation, as Isaac looked and waited eagerly for the arrival of his new bride. (Gen. 24:63.)

As Christians we have so much to look forward to: 1) the salvation of our families, 2) the evangelization of the world, 3) the reviving of our churches, and, 4) most of all, that blessed hope, the return of Christ the Bridegroom for His Bride, the Church.

"For I know the plans I have for you," declares the Lord, "plans to prosper you and not to harm you, plans to give you hope and a future" (Jer. 29:11 *NIV*). What a future we have to look forward to!

". . . 'Not by might nor by power, but
by My Spirit,' says the Lord of hosts."
Zechariah 4:6 NKJ

Not by **might**. The word **might** in the original Hebrew has to do with military strength. In Bible days Israel was not a war-like nation. Its rural lifestyle consisted of peaceful farming and herding of sheep and goats.

The Lord was the Israelites' defense, and they knew it. As God's people walked in obedience and trust, He defended them time after time. This verse reminded them that victory is not assured by massive numerical strength. Although they had warriors to defend them, just as we have the military today to protect us, they knew that the Lord was their real security: **. . . except the Lord keep the city, the watchman waketh but in vain** (Ps. 127:1).

Nor by **power**. Whereas *might* is a team word, *power* refers to what one person can do. It has to do with native ingenuity, with putting one's nose to the grindstone, one's shoulder to the wheel. It implies single-handedly taking the initiative and pushing past all opposition. It is a word which speaks to loners who would rather do things alone than to work with others. Soloists, lone rangers, prima donnas, and superstars like the word *power* because it glorifies the individual.

But this message from the Lord says that it is neither by the might of men nor by the power of any one person that you and I are kept. Our security is solely dependent upon God's Spirit. We are reminded that with the Lord there is no restraint to save by many or by few. (1 Sam. 14:6.) Our reliance is not on numerical strength or human cleverness. Our reliance is on the Lord!

Until the time that his word came to pass, the word of the Lord tested him.
Psalm 105:19 NKJ

Tried by the Word. Tested by a promise from the Lord. Joseph was 18 years of age when the Lord gave him the promise of a miraculous ministry. Joseph waited 12 long years for the fulfillment of that promise. The waiting period was not easy, but he had a promise to cling to. That very promise tried him as a person. The Hebrew word translated **tried** in this verse means "to purify and refine." It is a term used to describe the removing of impurities from gold ore in order to produce pure metal. The Word of God refined and purified Joseph.

Many Christians are taught that God uses circumstances to purify and refine them. There is a suffering cult which holds that human misery has redemptive value. "Suffer and win points with God," they seem to say. Jeremiah would not agree, because he says of God: . . . **He does not afflict willingly, nor grieve the children of men** (Lam. 3:33 NKJ).

It was not circumstances which tested Joseph and refined him, it was the promise of God. His adverse circumstances cried out, "No way." But the promise came back emphatically: "There shall be a performance of those things promised you by the Lord." (Luke 1:45.)

When your situation contradicts the promises and assurances God has given you, you have two choices: you can confess the circumstance or confess the word of promise. Remember: circumstances can change, but the Word of God will never change. Like Joseph, you can live to see a beautiful fulfillment of all those things promised you by the Lord. (Num. 23:19.)

. . . the Lord Himself will descend
from heaven with a shout . . . .
1 Thessalonians 4:16 NKJ

Israel of old had three kinds of shouts. All three could adequately be represented in this particular verse.

First, there was a vintage shout. During the period of the judges, Hebrew life was very precarious. Due to the uncertainties of life, no one was really sure of seeing a crop all the way through from planting seed to threshing grain. Gathering in a bountiful harvest became a cause for rejoicing. In our verse, Jesus could be giving a vintage shout because the harvest of souls is finally being reaped and gathered into the garner. (James 5:7.)

Israel also had a nuptial shout. This happy, joyful shouting occurred during wedding festivities. (Is. 62:5.) At His coming to redeem His Bride, the Church, and to proclaim the wedding feast of the Lamb, Christ may give forth a nuptial shout of joy.

Finally, there was a shout of war. This was the jubilant war cry given during battle in confident anticipation of victory. In the original Greek text, the word translated **shout** is *keleuma (kel'-yoo-mah)* or "shout of war." It includes *incitement* (**"Gather My saints together to Me . . . ."** (Ps. 50:5 *NKJ*) and *command* ("Satan, step aside, I am coming through your territory to receive My Church!").

The Second Coming of Christ will involve conflict, but *once* the Lord leaves heaven and descends with the shout of victory, the battle is over right then. The next verse joyfully declares, . . . **And thus we shall always be with the Lord** (v. 17 *NKJ*). Hallelujah!

"In My Father's house are many mansions . . . ."
John 14:2 NKJ

Have you ever wondered what heaven is like? Since we believers will be there for all eternity, it does seem that we should give some thought to our future home. Our stay on earth is transient, while our dwelling in eternity is called our **long home** (Eccl. 12:5). Jesus described that "home" as a mansion. The Greek word used here is *mone (mon-ay')*, which has a lot of interesting possibilities worth considering.

Out of the economic depression of the 1930s there came the "mansion mentality." Many of God's people, having lost all hope of ever prospering in this life, began to dream of one day moving into stately and ornate dwellings. "Mansion songs" sprang up during this time as a reassurance to the numberless earth-bound vagabonds that their eternal destiny was a place of dazzling white palaces — much like the antebellum "Southern" mansions they saw portrayed in Depression-era movie epics such as *Gone With the Wind*.

We should not discount entirely the hope of a residence that will far exceed in stateliness and beauty anything we have ever lived in on earth. However, *mone* carries with it a connotation not of stability, but of mobility. Some lexicographers have defined it as "way-stations on the journey," or as "stopping places along the road." Heaven could easily be a place of unfolding vistas, horizons, plateaus, and new sights.

Thus Jesus' use of the word *mansion* suggests rest in the midst of continual progressive activity. What He might have been saying was: "In My Father's house are many way-stations where you will stop in between the continuous unfolding of God's eternal purpose."

> . . . **all the children of Israel**
> **had light in their dwellings.**
>
> **Exodus 10:23** NKJ

What a study in contrasts! Egyptian homes shrouded with darkness like a blanket — darkness so thick you could almost cut it with a knife. By contrast, all the children of Israel flooded with light in their dwellings. Using the symbolism we find in Scripture, Egypt is a type of the world system. Israel is a type of the Church. This verse is thus telling us that believers walking in the light of truth will carry that light right into their homes. Likewise, those following the prince of darkness will live in homes which are an extension of that darkness.

This promise assures you and me of light in our dwellings, regardless of world conditions. The ending of the Church Age is likened to a setting sun. Jesus said that He was working while it was yet day because the night was coming when no man could work. (John 9:4.) It is evening time for the Church. In Zechariah 14:7, the Lord promises that His followers will have light even in the evening of life. We who believe will be bathed in light even when the sun is setting upon the world.

According to Esther 8:16, light in the dwelling is accompanied by gladness, joy and honor. Not only is the home of the believer assured illumination, but also a general profusion of God's blessings. It is possible, probable, and preferable that our homes be so filled with the presence of the Lord that all non-Christians visiting there will be touched and impressed with that light. It can happen!

"That He would show you the secrets of wisdom! For they would double your prudence . . . ."

Job 11:6 NKJ

Here is a word from the Lord that links the best of two realms. It blends natural skills, understanding and expertise with supernatural insight. It is the Lord's way of adding the wisdom from above to the natural common sense and native ability He has given each of us. God's superior knowledge coupled with our natural human instinct produces an unbeatable combination.

This verse is especially vital to salesmen, executives, factory foremen, employers, business owners, and all those who must compete daily in the market place of life. Our God is telling us to be knowledgeable, informed, aware. Each of us needs to know everything he can find out about his occupation if he expects to succeed in this competitive world. The Christian has to think faster and better than the competition if he is to survive. The non-Christian's thinking is pre-occupied with self-aggrandizement. The Christian, on the other hand, has a clear channel to wisdom because the Holy Spirit of God has shown him how to get the victory over selfishness.

Here, the Lord is promising to add His knowledge, understanding, insight and expertise to ours. That gives us a double portion of wisdom — or what one translator calls "two-sided wisdom."

Make this fourfold confession of faith: "With God's wisdom I can have: 1) twice the results with half the effort, 2) the competitive edge over the non-Christian, 3) a doubled output, and 4) a double portion of God's blessing on my life and work." Praise the Lord!

**"They shall be Mine," says the Lord of hosts,
"On the day that I make them My jewels . . . ."**
Malachi 3:17 NKJ

This verse has always stirred my imagination to visualize a great circle of celestial beings gathered around the throne of God. The throne is majestic and awesome because the Lord God of Hosts is seated on it. Around Him all the angels are in attendance and the whole heavenly assembly stands and gazes with rapture upon the power center of the universe.

I also visualize a circle of redeemed saints encompassing the throne like a great rainbow. The beautiful and most breathtaking aspect of this magnificent assembly is the fact that the circle is unbroken. The reason it is complete is because God's will has been finally done on earth as it is in heaven.

The Lord's promise that all those who are to come to know Him will be there on the day He makes us His jewels has guaranteed the completion of the circle of the redeemed. I know from Scripture, however, that not every person on earth will be there in that circle. I have met people who say they do not want to be there. God will not force them to come. He invites people to enter the Kingdom of heaven; He doesn't coerce them into it. But He does declare in His Word that His plan is for the salvation of the *whole* family. If there are members of your family who do not yet know the Lord, quote Malachi 3:17 aloud and make it part of your fourfold confession of faith: 1) "There is a circle around the throne of God." 2) "It is a family circle." 3) "It is my family circle." 4) "The circle will not be broken! All my family will be there!" Praise the Lord!

". . . I am the Lord, I do not change . . ."
Malachi 3:6 NKJ

This is an encouraging word for those seeking stability in a changing world. In the creation, God set up the succeeding seasons, the alteration of day and night, the incoming and outgoing tides. He placed man in a world in which the sun rises at a different time every single day and sets at a different time each evening.

Life is so filled with activity that we must constantly adjust, adapt, and accommodate ourselves to changing situations — even in nature. Behind all this ceaseless motion, there is one constant: God. Whatever may be going on about us, we can always know that He is the same, day in and day out. He can be depended on. He does not change. He is not fickle. He is not moody. He does not feel good about us one day and bad the next. His love is always steadily on course.

This verse can be especially helpful when we find ourselves in situations that seem rather shaky. We speak about having to walk on egg shells, tread on thin ice, or build on shifting sands. That kind of feeling does not give us much of a sense of stability.

The Scriptures liken the Lord to a rock. A rock is stable. It will be there after the storm has passed. Rain doesn't wash it away, lightning doesn't move it. This promise from our Creator, "I am the Lord, I change not," tells us that day after day He is "on the job." He never takes vacations, days off, or leaves of absence. Anytime, anywhere, under any circumstance, we can breathe His name and be assured of an instant audience with Him. What an encouragement to know that the Lord Who watches over His people neither slumbers nor sleeps. (Ps. 121:4.)

. . . **there shall enlargement and deliverance arise** . . . .
Esther 4:14

In this verse, the Lord promises us not only a deliverance from every dilemma, but also an enlargement in our particular calling and station in life. The text reverses their order, but for the sake of clarity I would like to present these two occurrences this way: 1) deliverance or liberation of a person from a temporary state of confinement, followed by 2) enlargement or expansion of his sphere of influence.

We see this sequence in the life of David. In his youth as a shepherd he slays a marauding bear. Reports of this incident reach his family. Next he overcomes a lion which is attacking the flock of sheep. A lion is more ferocious and destructive than a bear, so news of this exploit reaches all the shepherds.

Next David faces the giant, Goliath. He draws upon his past experiences to declare openly: "The Lord who delivered me from the paw of the bear and the lion will deliver me from the hand of this uncircumcised Philistine." Again David's enlargement grows. This time to the whole Israelite army. The Lord then rescues David from the hand of King Saul, enlarging his reputation in all of Israel and Judah. Finally, David becomes king himself and is delivered from an insurrection lead by Absalom, and his sphere of influence reaches the nations.

Every time you faithfully trust the Lord for His deliverance, two things happen: 1) He sets you free, and 2) He enlarges your potential. You will not stay in the same trying circumstances perpetually. You will come out, and with expansion. It is worth pursuing after deliverance in order to reap the reward of enlargement!

. . . **"Do not listen or consent."**
1 Kings 20:8 NKJ

King Ahab of Israel was being intimidated by a bully.
Ben-hadad was putting fear in his heart by threatening to
move into Israel, take over Ahab's kingdom, and carry off
all his possessions. Fearfully Ahab offered no resistance, but
instead caved in to Ben-hadad's outrageous demands. Ahab's
spineless reply was: "Just as you say, all that I have is yours."

The elders of the land responded differently. "'Do not
listen or consent,'" they advised Ahab. "You're listening to
the wrong voice. You're accepting what you should be refus-
ing."

We receive mail from people who have recurring
nightmares. Usually their dreams are about accidents,
injuries, or personal harm coming to loved ones. My
response is always to send them this verse, urging them to
take a stance of refusal and denial. I remind them that as
believers related to the Lord, we are told to yield no
topography or ground to the enemy.

One time, our family was scheduled to take a trip over
a treacherous mountain road. Three times I dreamed that
we had an accident at a certain bad curve on that road. After
the third time, I quoted this verse, declaring: "This could
happen, but it doesn't have to. I don't believe an accident
would glorify God or serve any useful purpose. Since it has
no utility, I refuse that dream in Jesus' name!" We made the
trip both ways with no problem.

You can do the same thing with negative dreams,
visions, or apprehensions. Refuse to receive them!

. . . You brought us out to rich fulfillment.
Psalm 66:12 NKJ

This term **rich fulfillment** is translated from a Hebrew word *revayah (rev-aw-yaw')* meaning total satisfaction. This word is derived from a primitive root word *ravah (raw-vaw')* which means "to slake the thirst," or "to abundantly satisfy the appetite."

David lists the trying circumstances he and the people of Israel had faced and how the Lord had led them through all their difficulties. He relates how the enemy had tried to enslave them, to submerge them, to overcome them with fire and flood. But then he tells of the Lord's gracious dealings with him and his people:

"Because of You, Lord, we are actually better off now than we were before our trial. We held on to Your promises and You fulfilled them all. You gave us the courage to endure, led us through the tests, and then rewarded us by bringing us out to total satisfaction."

Sometimes a greater insight into a word can be gained by comparing it with other usages in the Scriptures. *Revayah* appears one other time in the Old Testament: in Psalm 23:5 where David declares of the Lord's blessings, **. . . my cup runneth over.** The word translated "runneth over" and "rich fulfillment" are one and the same (*revayah*). Moisture, satisfaction, and abundance are all embodied in this one word.

Never give up. The effort it takes to get through trying situations is always worth it when you come out to the **wealthy place** (*KJV*). Satan wants to discourage you into quitting and missing the blessing. Jesus wants you to persevere, to get past the place of difficulty, and to come out to *revayah,* the place of rich fulfillment. The effort is worth it!

. . . knowledge is easy to him who understands.
Proverbs 14:6 NKJ

The Lord is omniscient; He knows *all* things. In His Word He has promised to make available to His children all the treasures of His wisdom and knowledge. Our tendency is to complicate matters and make it difficult to obtain divine knowledge. This verse assures us that knowledge is easy for the person who understands the ways of God.

One time I was walking through a public place of business headed for a conference room where I was to take part in a seminar. Suddenly I noticed a man sitting all alone. Instantly the Lord put it on my heart to witness to the man about the love of God. I have a natural reluctance to go up to people I don't know and start talking. I did have a burden for the man and knew that the Lord was putting him on my heart. My spirit was saying to me, "Share God's love with him," but my flesh was saying, "But you don't even know this man!"

Inwardly I was praying for help. In answer to my prayer, the Lord imparted the knowledge about the man that I needed in order to approach him. Knowledge is factual. The Lord gave me the complete facts about the man's situation, his occupation, his relationship with his wife and children, and his attitude toward God. The man was so overwhelmed with my knowledge and concern that he broke into tears and surrendered his life to the Lord then and there.

The knowledge you need to be an effective witness is available. It is easy to come by. Jesus said that His yoke was easy. (Matt. 11:30.) Teamed with Him in service, His knowledge easily becomes your knowledge!

March 24

Commit your works to the Lord, and
your thoughts will be established.
Proverbs 16:3 NKJ

To "commit your works to the Lord" is to "roll" onto Him all your plans and schemes. It means to come to the place where you are willing to trust yourself and your future totally to His keeping, watchful care.

Before you and I became Christians, we learned self-preservation from the world system. Before conversion we thought we had to depend upon a survival instinct based on human cleverness and native ingenuity. It is quite a transition from "Look out for Number One" to "The will of the Lord be done." To get from self-will to God's will takes quite a bit of doing. This verse was placed in the Bible just to help us make the necessary adjustments to our attitude and actions.

Rolling your plans and activities onto the Lord can be done only when you are convinced that He is more interested in your happiness and well-being than you are. *The Amplified Bible* translates the promise of this verse: **. . . [He will cause your thoughts to become agreeable to His will, and] so shall your plans be established and succeed.**

Your thoughts are the equivalent of your plans, aims, objectives, hopes, and desires. Turn your future over to the Lord 100 percent, and then you can *know* that your plans will succeed. It is a paradox: hold on too tightly and you lose, release to the Lord and you win! Try it!

". . . You have cast all my sins behind Your back."
Isaiah 38:17 NKJ

This verse has universal appeal to everyone who has experienced genuine sorrow for sins committed. When we confess our sins to God, not only is He faithful and just to forgive us our sins (1 John 1:9), He also removes them from us and puts them behind His back.

All through Scripture we find references to the face of the Lord and the eyes of the Lord. For example, the prophet Habakkuk said of his God: **You are of purer eyes than to behold evil, and cannot look on wickedness** (Hab. 1:13 *NKJ*).

So confessed sins are removed from us and also from God's gaze by a process that puts them out of sight forever. Since God puts our sins out of His mind and view, we need to learn to do the same. Yet I continually meet people whom God has forgiven, but who have never forgiven themselves. That is not only tragic, it is also unnecessary — and spiritually unproductive.

Don't keep punishing yourself and carrying a load of self-imposed guilt when simple repentance and confession of sin removes completely and forever all condemnation and feelings of failure.

Since God is omnipresent — filling all of heaven and earth with His presence (Jer. 23:24) — we may ask where His "back" is? The answer is: In the opposite direction from His face and eyes. This verse lovingly assures us that the sins we have confessed to our heavenly Father are no longer visible to Him. What blessed release!

". . . for every idle word men may speak, they will give account of it on the day of judgment."
Matthew 12:36 NKJ

Put your words to work for you! Speak words that produce action, results, or wages. This word *idle* is quite interesting. In the original New Testament writings, it is *argos (ar-gos')*. In the Greek, *a* is a privative negative, or as we say, an "un" word. *Ergos* refers to toil, labor, or any activity or work that pays wages.

Thus, "idle" words are words that are non-working, unemployed, inactive — words having no utility. Jesus used the word *argos* in the parable of the laborers in the vineyard in which the owner asked the eleventh-hour workers, "Why have you been standing here *idle* all day?" In other words, "Why are you not gainfully employed when there is work to be done?"

This verse is not an indictment against a sense of humor. Some Christians are so somber, joyless, and legalistic that they resent happy, joyful, or humorous people. Idle words are not anecdotes, aphorisms, metaphors, maxims, proverbs, or humorous stories.

Idle words are words that are unproductive. Since death and life are in the power of the tongue (Prov. 18:21), we are challenged to speak only words that generate life. Fill your mouth with praises. Let your speech be full of the promises of God. Every time you quote a scripture at the prompting of the Holy Spirit, you are releasing faith. With careful attention, your words can be fully active, fully employed, fully working.

"But others fell on good ground and yielded a crop: some a hundredfold, some sixty, and some thirty."

Matthew 13:8 NKJ

The context of this verse seems to indicate three types of Christians with varying percentages of return on the seed of the Word of God planted in them. It implies that some have the capacity to produce a 100 percent return on God's investment, while others can only muster 60 percent, and others even less. Each person is thus thought to have his own *set* "personal production potential."

Some scholars, however, see in this verse a *progress* in the life of each believer. To them, this verse says that each of us has three phases in our Christian life: PHASE ONE is when we are babes in Christ; PHASE TWO is when we are young, growing servants and handmaids of the Lord; PHASE THREE is when we are mature saints, grown-up adult Christians. "Thirtyfold," or phase one, could include the blessings that accompany the New Birth. "Sixtyfold," or phase two, would refer to the blessings of growth, expansion, enlargement, and development into spiritual adulthood. "A hundredfold," phase three, would entail all the blessings that come with the patience, faithfulness, consistency, and endurance of our later years.

If so, then the famous and eagerly-sought instant "hundredfold return" on our giving would not be a "windfall profit" at all, but rather a "long-term capital gain"!

The encouraging thing about this progression is that it is on-going. Thank God right now for raising your "personal production potential" and preparing you for the next phase of your unfolding life and ministry.

> . . . bear fruit . . . bear more
> fruit . . . bear much fruit . . . .
> **John 15:1-8** NKJ

We are living in an age that wants instant results. Ours is a push-button society that is turned off by delays, slowdowns, or obstructions. We want our photos, our printing, our cleaning and our answers — right now!

In the story of the tortoise and the hare, we are more impressed with the rabbit than with the turtle because the rabbit is speedy. Like us, he's anxious to be "off and running." He appeals to us because he's a "shaker and mover," the type that "makes things happen."

The turtle, on the other hand, is just not "with it." He's a slow mover, a plodder, a "real stick-in-the-mud type." He has no "pizazz," generates no excitement, no glamour. He's just plain dull!

Lost in our comparisons is the fact that the lowly turtle won the race while the speedy rabbit never made it to the finish line.

There are dozens of books on the market these days on how to go from kindergarten to graduate level in one quantum leap. Even many Christians seem to want to go from spiritual babyhood to manhood in "one giant step."

By contrast, this verse indicates a "longevity mindset." First we bear fruit. Then as we persevere and faithfully continue, we bear more fruit. If we keep at it, ultimately we bear much fruit. I certainly don't mean to extinguish the fires of enthusiasm or spiritual desire. But the message remains the same: It's the long haul which counts. Time is on our side. Sooner or later faithfulness and consistency produce fruit, then more fruit, then much fruit. It's just a matter of time!

**". . . we will give ourselves continually
to prayer . . . ."**

Acts 6:4 NKJ

The key phrase here is **give ourselves continually.** It is a statement indicating great intensity and exertion. This is not a casual, ho-hum, business-as-usual type activity, but one involving concentration and determined effort. My only intent in defining this expression is to open the way for all of us to a more effective prayer life.

In the original Greek text, **give ourselves continually** is only one word: *proskartereo (pros-kar-ter-eh'-o).* It is a compound word made of two components: 1) *pros,* meaning "toward, in the direction of, forward, or pertaining to," and, 2) *kartereo,* meaning "endurance, strength, steadfastness, and power."

To "give oneself continually to prayer" is to engage in an activity requiring time, energy, commitment and disciplined effort. It demands prayer habits that are consistent, persistent, and insistent. *Proskartereo* has thus been defined as "persevering diligence," "close adherence to a task," "constant diligence in exercise," and "steadfast earnestness." It implies taking prayer very seriously and working at it very hard.

One great writer on the subject of prayer has defined this expression as "making a business of prayer; surrendering oneself totally to prayer; putting fervor, urgency, perseverance, and time into prayer."

If your own prayer life does not match these descriptions, begin today to "give yourself continually to prayer." It is never too late to begin!

So the word of the Lord grew mightily and prevailed.
Acts 19:20 NKJ

The book of Acts makes three progressive statements about the Word of the Lord:

PHASE ONE is found in Acts 6:7 in which we read that in the infancy of the Church, the Word of God **increased.** This is what happened to us at our conversion. Before we came to know the Lord, our knowledge of Scripture was quite limited. Upon our conversion, however, an awakening to the beauty of the Word of God stimulated an appetite for more. In our Christian walk, His Word increases in us as we become more and more enamored with His marvelous promises.

PHASE TWO is found in Acts 12:24 which tells us that the Word of God **grew and multiplied** (*NKJ*). Applying this verse to ourselves, we experience an expanding consciousness of scriptures through an on-going, on-growing practice of daily studying the Word of God. The multiplying of that Word comes as we share it with others.

PHASE THREE is found here in Acts 19:20 where we read that the Word of the Lord **grew mightily and prevailed** (*NKJ*). In the original Greek, these words denote dominion and force. They are indicative of a heavily armed military unit triumphing in combat, driving out the enemy, and occupying territory as a conqueror with a great show of force.

As we grow in the Lord, we can experience: 1) an increase in knowledge of scriptures, 2) a normal growth in ability to multiply that knowledge by sharing it with others, and 3) a relationship with the Lord in which His Word becomes the one motivating factor of life.

Let this mind be in you which was also in Christ Jesus.
Philippians 2:5 NKJ

The key word in this sentence is **mind**. In the original
Greek, it is *phroneo (fron-eh'-o)* and covers a wide range of
meanings. Each definition of *phroneo* can speak volumes to
us.

In *The Amplified Bible* this word is translated "attitude."
We are urged to let the same attitude that Christ displayed
govern our activities. Jesus came to earth to do His Father's
will. He showed forth that purpose when He prayed:
. . . not my will, but thine, be done (Luke 22:42). He
attributed all His activities to a desire to please His Father.
We can have the same attitude.

Phroneo can also be translated "opinion." We can have
the same opinion about life that Jesus had. He loved truth.
So can we. He detested hypocrisy. We too can be turned off
by plastic artificiality. We can have His opinion of right and
wrong. If we will, we can let the same opinion be ours which
was in Christ Jesus.

Finally, *phroneo* can also be translated "interest" or
"motivation." We can be interested in and motivated by the
same things which interested and motivated Jesus Christ.
Our Lord was motivated to pray, to attend the house of God,
to fellowship with God's people, to care for the needy, and
to go about doing good. (Acts 10:38.) We too can allow the
same motivation to be in us which was in our Lord and
Savior. He is our role model.

The old hymn expresses this attitude, opinion, interest
and motivation best when it declares: "All I ask is to be like
Him."

April 1

. . . the peace of God . . . will guard your hearts and minds through Christ Jesus.

Philippians 4:7 NKJ

This verse calls to mind an armed sentinel standing by to prevent intrusion. Soldiers guard fortresses; sentries watch over premises. But here it is peace which stands guard. Peace does not seem militant enough to do any "guarding," yet it is God's choice to protect our hearts and minds.

The Greek word translated **peace** here is *eirene (i-ray'-nay)*. It includes the idea of joining and reconciling forces or factors to produce quietness, harmony, and unity. *Eirene* says: "Be reconcilied with God, and you will have rest and contentment. All division, disunity, distrust, and disruption will be removed when peace intervenes and takes over."

The lexicographers tell us that *eirene* implies more than concord, harmony, or just getting along with one's neighbor. Included in this word is the idea of security, safety, prosperity, and happiness. Your thoughts and affections can be in perfect harmony and you can enjoy total rest — all because of Jesus.

The verse adds the name of the Lord like a signature on a check. A check without a signature is worthless. Jesus gives validity to this promise by adding His name to it.

Peace not only guards heart and mind, but also reconciles both areas. Sometimes your heart will tell you one thing and your mind another. Pray for God's peace to reconcile the divided factions and bring them together. O happy times when heart and mind are in one accord!

**God also bearing witness both with signs
and wonders, with various miracles, and
gifts of the Holy Spirit . . . .**

Hebrews 2:4 NKJ

Just when you feel your witnessing is ineffective, your
testimony discredited, your words falling on deaf ears, the
Lord comes to add His testimony and witness to yours. This
action gives instant credibility to your Christian witness.

The Greek word translated **bearing witness** here is a
triple compound: *sunepimartureo (soon-ep-ee-mar-too-reh'-o)*. It
is composed of three elements: *sun* ("alongside"), *epi* ("in
addition to"), and *martureo* ("to witness and testify"). Thus
this verse says that if you will give your testimony to an
unbelieving world, the Lord will come alongside and add
His witness and testimony to yours. When the Lord bears
witness, it will be with signs, wonders, diverse miracles, and
gifts of the Holy Spirit. Supernatural confirmation is thus
promised you.

In the original Greek, the expression **gifts** is *merismos
(mer-is-mos')* which is defined as "distribution, division,
portion." We can be in a position where the Lord will
distribute to us a share of His miraculous and supernatural
power. At conversion, He gives each of us a measure of faith.
John 3:34 indicates that the Holy Spirit comes without
measure, but apparently His gifts are apportioned and
measured out individually as the Lord sees fit.

Our verse reassures us that if we will give our testimony,
the Lord will come and corroborate our witness by distribu-
tions of the Holy Spirit's ministry. Have you claimed your
share? If not, do so right away!

April 3

casting all your care upon Him, for He cares for you.
1 Peter 5:7 NKJ

This verse contains a play on words: your care becomes God's care. Reading in the original language helps add a dimension not always evident in the English version. The words "care" and "cares" in this verse happen to be two entirely different words. Looking closely at their meanings makes this promise even more precious to us.

In the Greek text, this word translated **care** is *merimna (mer-im-nah)*. It is a noun which has to do with anxiety, stress, distraction, preoccupation with insecurity, or worry. It suggests the kind of thoughts that trouble us and keep us from peace of mind. Jesus used this word when He said to His disciples: **. . . take no** (anxious) **thought for your life . . . .** (Matt. 6:25). This is a reminder that time spent worrying is wasted time, and so unnecessary. The time spent in anxiety could be better invested in Bible reading, prayer, praising the Lord, and waiting upon Him for direction.

The second word translated **cares** is *melo (mel-o)*, a verb meaning "to be concerned about or interested in." God is aware of you. He is interested in you. You can cast all your worries, anxieties, and insecurities upon Him because your well-being matters to Him.

Don't carry around any unnecessary burdens; the Lord invites you to shift them onto Him. He has a 2000-year head start on you when it comes to burden-bearing. He can be trusted. Give Him your cares; He cares!

" 'These things says He who is holy, He who
is true, ". . . *He who opens and no one
shuts, and shuts and no one opens":*

". . . See, I have set before you an open
door, and no one can shut it . . . .' "

Revelation 3:7,8 NKJ

This verse presents an area called *the transition zone.*

Think about the scene: Behind you is a door which the
Lord has closed. You know you cannot go back. There is
nothing to go back to. In front of you stands a door to new
opportunities, new challenges, new ministry, new spheres
of influence, a whole new future. In this transition zone in
which you find yourself, the door to the past is sealed shut,
but the door to the future has not yet opened. You know
the Lord is leading you to make the forward move. You know
it is time to progress. But, both doors remain securely closed
against you. There are all kinds of indications that the new
door will open, but so far you are at a standstill. What is
expected of you in this situation?

You must maintain a good level of trust in your God.
This is no time to oscillate, fluctuate, or vacillate. This is the
time to be reassured that the same Lord who closed the old
door behind you will also open the new door in front of you.
His leading you into the transition zone is not a sign of
abandonment, but of His confidence in you and of your need
of confidence in Him. Remember: He did not bring you out
to desert you; He brought you out in order to bring you in!
(Deut. 6:23.)

**This wisdom descendeth not from above, but
is earthly, sensual, devilish . . . . But the
wisdom that is from above is first pure . . . .**

James 3:15,17

There is a sentence in the Anglican prayer book that reads: "Deliver us from the world, the flesh, and the devil." That sentence was drawn from this verse in James. **Earthly** refers to the world. **Sensual** is the equivalent of the flesh. **Devilish** has to do with Satan and his demons. Verse 17 of this passage contains a reference to the true wisdom which is from above. Thus these verses deal with four kinds or sources of wisdom.

Earthly wisdom is centered in the human intellect. As beneficial as it may be to us in this life, since it deals with matters of time and not eternity, it does not adequately prepare us for the other world.

Sensual wisdom is centered in the human body. This wisdom comes to us through the senses and relates to the world of entertainment, advertising, art, fashion, and recreation. It appeals to the flesh or physical side of man. It too fails to equip for eternity.

Devilish wisdom is centered in the spirit realm. It can be found in horoscopes, Ouija boards, tarot cards, seances, and other spiritist activities. Its danger is that it leads people away from the truth of God and opens them up to the lies and deception of the enemy.

Wisdom from above is centered in the Holy Spirit. It is God-given wisdom. It originates from outside of man, but is available to him for the asking. (James 1:5.) The beautiful thing about this wisdom is that it is three-dimensional: with it we can be in good relationship with God, in good harmony with our fellowman, and at peace with ourselves.

. . . He has made us accepted in the Beloved.

Ephesians 1:6 NKJ

Accepted in the Beloved. What an encouraging word. In this world, with its constant search for affection, approval, and acceptance, it is good to know that we Christians are accepted in the Beloved. We do not have to struggle for acceptance, we already have it. How comforting to know that our Father will not love us any more (or less!) in the future than He does right now.

Sometimes the best way to understand a word is to find out how it is used elsewhere. This word *accepted* is no exception. In the original Greek text, it is *charitoo (khar-ee-to'-o)*, and is closely related to the grace word *charis*. *Charitoo* is defined as "highly favored," "graced with honor," and "accepted." It only appears one other time in the New Testament and that is in Luke 1:28 when the angel appeared to Mary and called her by this name: . . . **"Rejoice, *highly favored one*, the Lord is with you; blessed are you among women!"** (*NKJ*). The word used to tell Mary that she was highly favored by being selected by the Lord for a very special task is the same word used to describe all Christians. We have also been highly favored by being selected of God.

Mary was chosen to bring about the Lord's first coming into the world. All believers have been chosen to bring about the Lord's Second Coming into the world.

Quit putting yourself down. If you are a Christian, you are not an outcast, you are *charitoo* — accepted in the Beloved!

**who comforts us in all our tribulation, that we may
be able to comfort those who are in any trouble . . . .**
2 Corinthians 1:4 NKJ

This is a case of "freely you have received, freely give."
Each of us has received something from the Lord (in stress
situations) that we can pass on to others. This makes us a
channel of blessing.

In this verse, the Apostle Paul says that not only do we
receive comfort from the Lord, but that we can also pass
that comfort on to others. Comfort is that special
"something" the Lord imparts to us to sustain us, undergird
us, and reinforce us in times of trial and tribulation. The
very word itself paints an image of the Lord leaning over
the portals of heaven and calling out to us words of
encouragement and reassurance. He does even more than
that. He comes down and stands alongside of us to speak
words of comfort to us in our time of greatest need. Then
He tells us to do the same for others. Be a comforter, a
consoler, an encourager to those who have needs like your
own.

There are people in our world who feel that no one
understands what they are going through. Furthermore, they
are convinced that no one even cares. When you have been
comforted by the Lord, you can say to such people, "Look,
I understand what you are going through and I care, because
I have been there myself." It is by undergoing — and over-
coming — our own trials that we are made able to comfort
others in their times of testing. The Lord has comforted you
in your time of need; now pass that comfort on!

... "Some say ... Elijah, and others Jeremiah ... ."
Matthew 16:14 NKJ

Jesus had just asked His disciples how the world viewed Him. They relayed to their Master that people saw Him in different capacities. Some felt He was a reflection of Elijah, while others felt He was of the Jeremiah mold. The thing that is interesting here is that Jesus is a fine blend of many characteristics of both men which we would do well to emulate.

Elijah was Mr. Firm. He was as straight as an arrow. One of his many positive qualities was manliness. He was strong spiritually, physically, mentally, emotionally, and volitionally. Elijah comes across as a no-nonsense type with unusual strength of character, intense spiritual drive, and a determined will. The people saw these same qualities in Jesus when He refused to be intimidated by the religious leaders. It was easy to associate Jesus with Elijah because of His strength.

Jeremiah was the exact opposite. He was gentle, compassionate, kind, merciful, patient, genteel. He was known to weep openly, was highly sensitive, and had a great capacity for love and kindness. Like Jeremiah, Jesus was tenderhearted and possessed great feelings.

Put Elijah and Jeremiah together and you have a person who is tough but gentle, firm but compassionate, rugged and strong but blessed with great sensitivity. It would be good if each of us could incorporate these same qualities in our own life. We too need to be firm against sin, but compassionate with the sinner. What an ideal!

. . . But at evening time it shall . . . be light.
Zechariah 14:7 NKJ

This verse speaks of a phenomenon of light at evening. It refers to a future time when Jesus will bodily return to earth and His feet will touch down upon the Mount of Olives. According to verse 4, . . . **the Mount of Olives shall be split in two, from east to west, making a very large valley . . . .** In the midst of all the descriptions of things which will then come to pass, we find these words of comfort, "And at evening time, it will be light." What would ordinarily be a time of the setting of the sun will, instead, become a scene of great illumination.

In the Bible, the Gospel era is likened to a day. Sunrise is a type or symbol of Pentecost when new light shone down upon the disciples and the birth of the infant Church ushered in the dawn of a bright new day. Noon time is like the Middle Ages. It is the heat of the day, a time of scorching sun, a moment of slowed activity and lessened productivity. Three p.m. is like the Reformation period. The 4 p.m. time is like the evening breeze or the revival times of the last days. Genesis 3:7 calls this period the cool of the day.

Evening time, sunset, or suppertime is like the ending of the Church Age. This Scriptural promise of phenomenal brightness at day's end assures us that we can be bathed in light all the way up to the Lord's coming. The sun will set on civilization, but we who look for His coming will be lit with the glory of the Lord. Cheer up, your light has come! (Is. 60:1.)

**My flesh and my heart fail; but God is the
strength of my heart and my portion forever.**

Psalm 73:26 NKJ

This verse was visibly demonstrated to me in an
intensive care unit. Leitha, a friend of the family, was rushed
to the hospital suffering from a severe heart attack. Hovering
between life and death, she was being monitored closely
by the hospital staff. The machine attached to her showed
a dot and a wavy line, a dot and a wavy line. It was explained
to me that this was an indication that the heart beat was
normal and that Leitha was resting comfortably.

Due to the serious nature of Leitha's condition, the nurse
in attendance limited my wife and me to a visit of five
minutes or less. She also expressed a great concern that any
"excitement" could cause Leitha irreparable damage. For four
minutes my wife and I carried on the normal social amenities
with Leitha. How are you? Are you eating? Are you resting
well? All the time we were talking, I kept watching the
monitor. There it was, steady as a clock: dot, wavy line; dot,
wavy line.

With one minute to go, I quoted Psalm 73:26.
Immediately the lines on the monitor jumped. They began
to go up and down, even disappearing off the top and
bottom of the screen. Quickly the nurse hurried us out of
the room thinking that Leitha was going to die from the
sudden burst of excitement. A few days later, however, Leitha
was released from the hospital, completely healed. Those
lines running up and down and off both top and bottom
of the monitor were visible proof that God's Word is living
and powerful, able to penetrate joints and marrow. We saw
it with our own eyes!

> **. . . thine enemies shall be found liars unto**
> **thee; and thou shalt tread upon their high places.**
> **Deuteronomy 33:29**

He was in tears and visibly shaken by his circumstances. He was the proprietor of a local doughnut shop and had been doing well until trouble came his way. An unscrupulous person came into his store and staged a phony accidental fall. Right behind the "injured party" was a person with a camera to take a picture of the "accident." Behind that person was another man ready to take down the names of convenient "witnesses." A lawsuit for an exorbitant sum of money was then filed by the "victim" who had staged the whole scenario.

This dear brother told me, "Dick, I could lose it all. My insurance policy for this type of accident is minimal at best. If this fellow wins this case, I could lose everything I own." I stood in agreement with the shopkeeper, praying with him that the Lord would work a miracle of deliverance. How I appreciate the faithfulness of the Lord in these situations. I was not familiar with Deuteronomy 33:29, but the Holy Spirit quickened it to me: "All your enemies shall be found as liars unto you."

The next day, in his private chambers, the judge in charge of the case began to read over the records. The trial was to start in one hour. Suddenly the magistrate was heard to make this statement in disgust: "This is a travesty of justice. The plaintiff is obviously a pathological liar. I refuse to hear this case. I am throwing it out of court."

An overnight fulfillment of a word from the Lord! Case dismissed! Another enemy found as a liar!

How should one chase a thousand, and two put ten thousand to flight, except their Rock had sold them . . . ?
Deuteronomy 32:30

You and I really do not need another sermon on the necessity and value of unity and teamwork. Common sense tells us that cooperation is vital to accomplishment. We know there is a great need for people to work together for the good of the cause. It is the actualization of what we already know about unity that is needed now.

One can stand against a thousand discouraging things, but two can stand against ten thousand. Having another person alongside to help increases one's potential by nine thousand. That should be a great incentive for working harmoniously with others. As I travel widely, I am constantly meeting Christians who are getting the exact same word from the Lord: *cooperation.* Christianity is not for soloists, prima donnas, lone rangers, heavyweights, or superstars. The Body of Christ is one unit, but it is made up of many components. None of us is a law unto himself or herself. We must work together as a team to represent Christ to the uncommitted. Just as the world needs us, so we believers need each other.

Our Lord has promised to bless cooperation. Alone you or I can push back a thousand obstacles. Together we can push back ten thousand. The more we cooperate, the higher the percentage of results. By taking this promise to heart, we can go from "fruitfulness" (John 15:2) to "much fruitfulness." (John 15:5.) Let's do it!

Why was not this ointment sold for three hundred pence, and given to the poor?
John 12:5

Mary is remembered for breaking an alabaster box and anointing Jesus for burial with costly spikenard ointment. Judas Iscariot was critical of the action, placing a cash value of 300 pence on the contents. Since one pence was a day's wage, Mary was actually pouring on Jesus the equivalent of a year's salary.

In the parable of the vineyard, the employer . . . **agreed with the labourers for a penny a day** . . . . (Matt. 20:2). When Jesus asked Philip how much it would cost to buy food for 5,000 people, Philip replied, . . . **Two hundred pennyworth of bread is not sufficient** . . . . (John 6:7). This does not equal two dollars, but 200 days' wages!

So Mary actually had, by Judas' evaluation, "wasted" 12 ounces (a Roman liter) of ointment which, if sold, could have brought in enough cash to feed 7,500 people. No wonder Judas' reacted as he did!

One sidelight of the incident: This "waste" to which Judas was referring is also translated "perdition." In Greek it is *apoleia (ap-o-li-a)*. Later when Judas had left to betray His Master, the Lord used this same word to describe His betrayer. He spoke of Judas as the son of "perdition" (*apoleia*). (John 17:12.) It may be some consolation to realize that when you are being criticized, invariably the things you are accused of are the exact same things your accusers are guilty of. Mary's act of devotion and love is branded a "perdition" by the very "son of perdition." That ought to take the sting out of the criticism you have been getting lately!

**. . . He who is in you is greater
than he who is in the world.**

1 John 4:4 NKJ

Someone once asked me why a football never gets deflated in a game. Twenty-two huge, burly men kick it, throw it, pounce on it, fumble it — yet it never gets "squashed" or loses its size to deflation. The answer is a simple law of physics. It seems that the internal pressure of the ball is much greater than all the pressure 22 men can place upon it externally.

This verse says the same thing about us as Christians. The power of the Holy Spirit residing in our hearts and lives is greater than all the pressure the external world can place upon us.

You could list all the different opponents who come against you to impede or block your forward progress. Satan's strategy is to deflate you and render you inoperative, but the Holy Ghost gives you a buoyancy. You can roll with the punches. It may seem sometimes that you are being tossed around by circumstances, but with the Lord's power within, you will always bounce back.

This verse is a great comfort to many people who are not having it very easy in life. It is a constant reminder of God's sustaining grace, Christ's resident peace, and the Holy Spirit's indwelling power. Greater is the power within us than the pressure upon us. So hang in there, teammate; despite the hard knocks, we're winning!

> **. . . he who waters will also be watered himself.**
> **Proverbs 11:25** NKJ

Our English language sometimes confines our understanding of Biblical principles. Twice in this verse we find a form of the word *water.* At face value, we could assume we are being told here that if we give someone a cup of water, then sooner or later someone else will give us a cup of water in return. That interpretation is only partially accurate.

This principle of reciprocity is found throughout the Bible. For example, **Give, and it shall be given unto you . . . .** (Luke 6:38); **Draw nigh to God, and he will draw nigh to you . . . .** (James 4:8). However, this verse promises far more than a simple "tit for tat." It has a greater dimension than reaping (*only*) what we have sown.

A look at a Hebrew-English lexicon will reveal that there are two different Hebrew words used here — both highly significant. The first word translated **waters** is *ravah (raw-vaw')* and has to do with satisfying a thirst. In Christian circles, this action would be the same as giving a person a cup of cold water in the name of the Lord.

The second Hebrew word translated **watered** is *yara (yaw-raw')*, meaning "to pour out like rain, descend like a shower, fill up by a deluge, flow like waters from a cloudburst."

So, with a little imagination, we could interpret this verse: "If you give someone a cup of cold water in the name of the Lord, He will pour out on you the whole reservoir!" What a promise!

**"...he who loves Me will be loved by My Father,
and I will love him and manifest Myself to him."**
John 14:21 NKJ

This is a very intimate promise. It speaks to those who want more than a shallow, superficial relationship with the Lord.

As I travel, I meet precious saints of God everywhere who say they want more out of life than what they are now experiencing. They have a yearning for a deeper, closer spiritual relationship with the Lord than what their church is able to provide. They are on a personal quest for "more" of the Lord. I pray that you, too, will sense that yearning and embark on that quest.

In this verse, Jesus is promising that to those who truly hunger and thirst for Him, He will manifest Himself personally. This manifestation is more than a conversion experience. It is more than a sanctification experience. It is even more than a baptism with the Holy Spirit. In addition to all these beautiful and dynamic encounters with the Lord, He is promising each of us a personal visitation.

In the original Greek text, this word translated *manifest* is *emphanizo (em-fan-id'-zo)*. It is a verb meaning "to disclose by appearance." Literally, it could be interpreted as "to shine within," "to exhibit plainly," or "to appear openly." All you need to receive such a disclosure is a heart-hunger for more of Jesus and His power and love. He will meet you in an individual way.

Blessed are you who hunger and thirst for righteousness. You shall be visited — and *soon*!

> . . . "The Lord is able to give
> you much more than this."
> **2 Chronicles 25:9** NKJ

How often are we willing to settle for less than God's best for our lives? Sometimes when a step of faith requires some real effort, it seems easier to give in to pressure and accept substandard arrangements or provision. This verse assures us that the Lord is trying to raise our sights in order to raise our levels.

Whatever you may have in life right now, the Lord is able to give you much more than this. His plans for you, if accepted and implemented by you, will improve your quality of life. Good will become better. Better will become best. God is able to do much more for you. Best of all, He is willing to do it. All it takes is faith.

But faith is not a struggle to convince your "spirit" of something your mind knows is really not so. It's not saying "I believe" over and over until you "psyche" yourself into believing by force of sheer repetition. Faith is not brain-washing or mouth wishing.

Simply stated, faith is nothing more than believing God. We have all heard of the great faith of Abraham. Yet what he did, we can all do: . . . **Abraham** *believed God,* **and it was counted to him for righteousness** (Rom. 4:3). Abraham became known as the "father of faith." Why? Because of his attitude and actions . . . **before him** *whom* **he believed, even God . . . .** (v. 17).

The Lord is able to give you much more than this. If you have faith — if you believe God — then take Him at His Word. Do what Abraham did: Believe God, agree with God, obey God. Do that, and you will receive "much more than this" from Him! Amen!

"...healing all who were oppressed by the devil."

Acts 10:38 NKJ

You have wanted more power in your life. You have desired to see more miracles in your ministry. You have fasted and prayed for a revival of signs, wonders, and miracles. One thing that will help speed the answer to those prayers is a clear understanding and appreciation of Satan's tyranny over the human race.

Jesus contested the malignancy of Satan and, by the powerful anointing of the Holy Spirit, healed the oppressed ones. The key word in this great description of Jesus' healing ministry is this reference to the oppression of the devil. The word *oppression* is defined as "domination, total control, tyranny, lordship; the exercise of authority over another person or persons as a potentate or dictator."

By their sin in the Garden of Eden, Adam and Eve abdicated their position as lords over the earth. By default, they surrendered their dominion and authority to the usurper, the prince of darkness, who now holds the unbelieving world in a cruel vise-like grip. (1 John 5:19 *NKJ*.) Jesus came to destroy the works of Satan. (1 John 3:8.) According to this verse in Acts, He went about doing good and breaking the stranglehold of Satan upon people.

In Psalm 97:10, David challenges us to love the Lord and hate the Evil One. You and I must look upon Satan's victims with great compassion, and at the same time hate the enemy for what he is doing to them. This will qualify us for miracles quicker than anything else we could ever do.

April 19

". . . sin lies at the door . . . ."
Genesis 4:7 NKJ

Here is another verse that has great potential for personal encouragement. The Lord is speaking to Cain and describing two conditions to him: 1) what happens if he does well (acceptance), and 2) what happens if he does not do well (a chance to make amends).

The usual interpretation of this verse is that sin is like a ravenous animal at the door ready to pounce on and devour the one who sins. But that is not what God is really saying here. Without getting too technical with the language, we can interpret the Hebrew word translated **sin** (*chatta'th*) (*khat-tawth'*) as a "sin *offering*." Thus this verse is really extending God's mercies to cover the failure areas of human life.

What the Lord was saying is: "Cain, if you do well, you will be accepted. If you do not do well, there is still a sin offering available for your reconciliation to Me. You don't have to go through life hounded by failure feelings, carrying a load of guilt and condemnation, defeated by your sins. There is a sin offering. Forgiveness can be yours. Reconciliation is to be preferred to alienation."

We do not have to go through life carrying the sin load. Jesus is our sin offering. He is the Lamb of God who takes away the sin of the world. (John 1:29.) Mercy triumphs over judgment. (James 2:13 NKJ.) This is good news for all of us. Doing good is great. Not doing good is tragic. But even then a way out has been provided. A sin offering is available. (Jesus bore our sins to free us from bondage to sin.) Call on the Lord and He will deliver you once and for all from guilt and condemnation. (Rom. 10:13.)

It is possible to give away (release) **and become richer! It is also possible to hold on too tightly and lose everything . . . .**
Proverbs 11:24 TLB

Here is a paradox. Letting go is enriching; holding on is impoverishing. It almost sounds the very opposite of everything we have ever been taught. Our crass world says: "Get all you can, and can all you get!" "Get while the getting is good!" "Opportunity only knocks once, so you'd better seize it when you get the chance!"

This verse is a confirmation of the Biblical admonition of Ecclesiastes 11:1 to "cast your bread upon the waters" (give to others), in confident assurance that "it will come back to you" (greatly multiplied).

While the Bible encourages thrift and preparation for emergencies (Prov. 22:3), it discourages unhealthy hoarding, insecure stockpiling, and anxiously awaiting some dreadful calamity.

Generosity is the key to prosperity, and outflowing is the key to contentment. Givers are fulfilled; takers are unfulfilled. The verse actually implies that giving people get richer while miserly people get poorer. Generous folks can always find something to give to worthy causes. Stingy folks find it extremely hard to find even a ten-cent piece for anybody else's welfare.

What a challenge to be generous! Give away and become richer. (It is the heavenly Father's nature to be giving.) Try it! You'll enjoy it! You're in for a very pleasant surprise when the full impact of this verse falls on you and its results start appearing in your life!

. . . the houses you broke down to fortify the wall.
Isaiah 22:10 NKJ

This verse warns us about being hollow on the inside and placing our whole emphasis on externals.

Israel was facing a seige. The enemy was pounding at the gates of Jerusalem and trying to demolish the city walls. In order to provide materials to use to fortify the outer defenses of the city, the people began dismantling their own houses. The walls were thus kept at the expense of private homes.

People in the world today will often do the same thing: sacrifice their home for a facade. Some people spend more time, energy, and money on external appearances than they spend on internal strengths and inner resources. You and I continually meet people who are hollow. They are empty inside. They have concentrated so much on putting up a good front (that is what this verse is all about) that they have never developed any real character or solid-quality integrity.

Happy the Christian who has Christ enthroned in his heart. He can say confidently, "Greater is He who is in me than he who is in the world."

Christ dwelling in our hearts enables us to be strong in the Lord and in the power of *His* might. We do not have to sacrifice inner resources to beef up external walls. We are strong both inside and outside. The Lord in our life makes the difference.

**If the ax is dull, and one does not sharpen
the edge, then he must use more strength . . . .**
Ecclesiastes 10:10 NKJ

Sometimes we have to make serious decisions that mean severing someone or something from our life. We painfully face the prospect of making unpleasant "cuts." A long-time employee must be released. A major household move has to be undertaken. (Sometimes moving from one location to another is as disruptive to a family as chopping is to a tree.) A life-time behavior pattern has to be changed drastically. All these "cuts" are hard, but they don't have to be brutal or bloody.

This verse tells us that a sharp cutting edge makes the difference. Dullness means that our action done in the power of the flesh will not only require much more strength, but will also be messier.

Jesus prayed all night before making His greatest decisions or changes. You and I rush in with a dull axe and chop away, but it is preferable to face major "cuts" with spiritual preparation. Fasting and prayer will sharpen the cutting edge of our faithful action.

Sometimes removal of persons from our association is like a surgeon cutting away an abscessed part of the body. With skill and speed he makes a deft incision, removes the poisonous mass, closes up the wound, and lets the healing process begin. The sharper the cutting edge, the quicker the recovery.

This verse urges "sharpness" in removing unpleasant elements that are keeping our "tree of life" from becoming as healthy and vigorous as it should be. Prayer "sharpens" us up for even the distasteful things we are called to do.

I will stand upon my watch . . . .
Habakkuk 2:1

Watchmen on the wall were on the lookout for four things: 1) fires from brush areas reaching the city, 2) wild animals which lived in the jungle-like vegetation along the Jordan River and which steathily approached inhabited areas when driven out of their dens by flood, 3) invading armies which sometimes crawled into position under cover of darkness, and 4) the dawn.

Once the sun rose, the watchmen were relieved of their responsibility. Along with fire, wild animals, and enemy forces, the rising of the sun occupied the thoughts of the watchmen of ancient times.

Habakkuk had a great hunger and thirst for the sun of righteousness. He had spiritual longings and desires. More than anything else, he wanted to meet God. He had an intensity that drove him relentlessly in his pursuit of God's visitation. We learn a great lesson from Habakkuk. The Lord honored his quest and fulfilled his heart's desire. All because he was faithful at his post of duty.

"I will stand upon my watch." In other words, "I want the Lord so much I will not be satisfied until He comes and meets me." Going away is not the answer to your situation. Taking a sabbatical will not do it. Retreats, advances, seminars, and conferences all add something of value to life. But Habakkuk would tell us his answer came when the Lord visited him at his post where he stood guard with commitment and fidelity: "I will stand upon my watch. I will wait and see." The Lord answered Habakkuk. He will answer you. Stand upon your watch. Bloom where you are planted!

In a dream, in a vision of the night, when deep sleep falls upon men, while slumbering on their beds, then He opens the ears of men, and seals their instruction.

Job 33:15,16 NKJ

Guidance while sleeping. Does that sound mystical? Esoteric? Metaphysical? Does it sound practical? Are you willing to trust God to provide you with guidance and direction while you are sound asleep?

This verse is meant to assist people who are facing major decisions, but who must cope with myriad distractions. You have a serious decision to make. The phone is ringing off the wall. People are continually asking you, "What are you going to do? Have you made up your mind yet? Which way are you going to go?"

You have the heavy responsibility of making the right decision. You also have a lot of pressure placed upon you by those around you who want to know what you are going to do. If that is your situation right now, take heart. This verse promises divine assistance in the whole matter.

Here the writer assures us that God is going to speak to us. In a dream. In a vision. In the night when deep sleep falls upon us, He will open our ears to hear. He will seal up our instruction. He will even warn us if we need warning. All this through the sleep process.

When the phone rings incessantly and all you hear is, "What are you going to do?" your response should be, "Sleep on it!" Good answer!

> **. . . the God of peace will crush
> Satan under your feet shortly . . . .**
> **Romans 16:20** NKJ

Two key phrases here are **crush** and **under your feet.**

In the original Greek, the word translated **crush** is *suntribo (soon-tree´-bo)*, meaning "to shatter, annihilate, torpedo, disintegrate, totally demolish." This verse assures us that God has a victory in store for us in every testing area of our lives. That victory will be so complete, the enemy will never again try to put that particular obstacle in our pathway.

Take heart! You have been assured that the victory your God has planned for you is so tremendous your enemy is going to be sorry he ever bothered you in the first place! Your triumphant deliverance is going to be such an embarrassment to the enemy that he wouldn't dare try the same tactic the second time to oppose you!

In Romans 1:17 Paul writes that we believers will go "from faith to faith" — from *victory* to *victory!*

Under your feet indicates that you and I must actively engage in the good fight of faith. To do that, we must go forth in battle array. Part of the armor of God which we wear is the covering for our feet. (Eph. 6:15.) We need that covering to tread on serpents and scorpions in the name of the Lord. (Luke 10:19.) It's worth it, because every place the sole of our foot trods on is ours! (Josh. 1:3.)

Get your marching shoes out! Get ready to tread down fear, insecurity, poverty, sickness, trouble, discouragement, and all the other works of the enemy. The God of peace is about to shatter Satan's opposition under our feet. Let's go! Onward Christian soldiers!

. . . the spirit indeed is willing, but the flesh is weak.
Matthew 26:41

There is a real study in contrasts in the words *willing* and *weak*. One describes a forwardness, the other a backwardness. One denotes eagerness, the other reticence. One is forthright and aggressive, suggesting taking the initative; the other is reluctant and apathetic, implying indecisiveness or a lack of ability. Let's take a closer look at each word individually:

The Greek word translated **willing** in this verse is *prothumos (proth'-oo-mos)*. The Greek prefix *pro* means "in front of" or "ahead of." *Thumos* refers to passion, ardor, enthusiasm, hard breathing. Thus, *prothumos* is a description of the spirit of man activated and energized by the Holy Spirit. In that case, we could say, "The spirit indeed is ready, alert, forward, eager, prompt, willing; the flesh is not."

The **flesh** is a good description of human nature or the qualities man inherited from Adam. You would think that with all his other improvements, man would have learned to sharpen his spiritual capacities. Not so. In John 6:63, Jesus says: "The flesh (human nature) profits nothing; it is the spirit that quickens and makes alive." Paul tells us in Galatians 5:17 that the fleshly man and the spirit man are at war with each other.

The word translated **weak** is *asthenes (as-then-ace')*, meaning "impotent" or "powerless." It is very close to the Greek word *asthma*, "shortness of breath." We could read this verse: "The spiritual man is breathing hard, eager and ready for action while the natural man is out of breath and unable to participate." To resolve this dilemma, we are told by Paul to walk in the spirit, and then we will not fulfill the tendencies of the flesh.

April 27

... there His power was hidden.
Habakkuk 3:4 NKJ

The original *King James Version* of this verse reads: **... there was the hiding of his power.** This passage describes a potency not visible to the human eye. It is a power that is not for public display, a power kept from the view of the mass of society.

Many believers long and pray for a ministry of the miraculous. Our world needs ministries which are accompanied by the supernatural evidences of miracles, signs and wonders. However, there is a danger in *seeking* these things. Unconsciously, prayers for manifest power usually imply huge crowds of people, amazing results, large offerings, great publicity, world-wide recognition and popularity. It seems that generally all of that "goes with the territory." Meet the needs of people, and they will come running. We see it in Jesus' ministry. He healed people, and the result was that multitudes followed Him.

But this verse declares that God also has a hidden power. That sobering fact causes us to ask ourselves some important questions about our motives in seeking divine power: Would I be willing to have God's power, and yet work behind a cloak of anonymity? Would I still seek a deliverance ministry if I knew it would mean spending the rest of my life in a mud hut in the jungle? Do I seek signs and wonders because they have become synonymous with "successful ministry"? Should miracle power ever be equated with popularity and fame?

Let us seek the "power gifts" for one reason only — not to magnify ourselves, but to bring glory to God by meeting human needs. Seeing God's power at work, whether conspicuously or inconspicuously, is reward enough!

April 28

Fulness is the key word here. In this verse, it is the Greek word *pleroma (play-ro-mah)*, which has an interesting sidelight.

When the ancients conducted a census of a city, if every dwelling place in it was occupied, then the town was listed as *pleroma*, fully occupied. When the crew of a ship attained full strength, it was listed as *pleroma*, indicating a full complement of officers and men. In addition, *pleroma* was used to describe a cargo net when it was "crammed full" of goods, or a hollow place which had been completely filled in. Inherent in its meaning also was the idea of a full-term of office or the completion of a task.

Paul's prayer is that you and I might be filled with all the fullness (the *pleroma*) of God Himself. We need this fullness in order to be able to complete our assigned tasks in life, to finish out our earthly service to the Lord. It is this fullness which will fill up the hollow places as yet unfulfilled in our human natures and characters. *Pleroma* will fill out our lives with God's surplus abundance. In turn, it will allow us to fill up God's crew on the old ship of Zion and, one day, to occupy our mansion and have our part in completing heaven's population.

To be filled with God is wonderful. To be filled with the fullness of God is super wonderful. To be filled with *all* the fullness of God has to be a mind-boggling experience. This *pleroma* was Paul's prayer for you and me. Let's receive it and enjoy it!

"The eternal God is your refuge, and
underneath are the everlasting arms . . . ."
Deuteronomy 33:27 NKJ

A *refuge* is a place of safety. In a game refuge, the animals
instinctively know they will not be trapped or shot at.
Likewise, we Christians have a refuge, a place of safety and
security from the traps and direct attacks of the enemy.

In speaking of this sense of security in the Lord, the
psalmist David wrote: **Great peace have they which love thy
law: and nothing shall offend them** (Ps. 119:165). In modern
versions, this word **offend** is usually translated "snare, trap,
capture." Thus, this is Biblical terminology for Satan's
attempts to capture believers and make them into prisoners
of fear, poverty, sickness, anger, lust, insecurity, etc.

In the original Hebrew, the word translated **refuge** here
is *me'ownah (meh-o-naw')*, meaning "a lair, den, asylum,
retreat, or home." As believers, our place of safety, of retreat,
of refuge from the assaults of the enemy, is the Lord God
of hosts.

Refuge *(me'ownah)* is also the word used for the taber-
nacle or temple where God dwells. We Christians have our
individual dwelling places, our *me'ownah*. God also has His
tabernacle, or *me'ownah* — His dwelling place. We not only
have the security of our own homes, but we also have an
added spiritual security in the place of worship. When we
worship the Lord in spirit and in truth, we find a beneficial
refuge from doubt, disbelief, distrust, despair, dismay, and
disturbance.

The Lord is our refuge: our lair, our den, our retreat,
our home, and our tabernacle!

. . . he who is of a merry heart has a continual feast.

Proverbs 15:15 NKJ

A feast is more than an ordinary meal. It includes the idea of company, music, entertainment, unusual or special gourmet foods. In general, a feast involves eating plus having a good time.

In our world, we see a great pursuit of "good times." People are trying so hard to find pleasure and satisfaction. You often hear the question, "Are we having fun yet?" The world is trying to find the right things in all the wrong places.

In John 4:32, the Lord Jesus told His disciples, . . . **"I have food to eat of which you do not know"** (*NKJ*). Our text verse confirms this truth. *The Amplified Bible* version reads: **. . . he who has a glad heart has a continual feast [regardless of circumstances].**

Believers do not have to spend a lot of money to go to a music concert. They have a song going on inside of them continuously. It is the song of the Lord. Jesus is singing it within their hearts. (Zeph. 3:17.) Christians don't have to wait up to hear some stand-up comedian on T.V. tell the latest jokes. They have the joy of the Lord within them giving them "a merry heart."

When the world comes up with a booklet called "How to Party Every Night of the Week," the Christian's response is, "I don't have to clutter my life with a lot of socializing; I'm so contented serving the Lord that I don't need partying."

The joy of the Lord is like a continuous feast. We are not anti-social, just contented and happy. We don't have to go around looking for what we have already found.

May 1

**He shall not be afraid of evil tidings:
his heart is fixed, trusting in the Lord.**

Psalm 112:7

Out of our twentieth-century culture there has come a familiar expression, "getting a fix." This term usually refers to taking drugs. Because of his dependency upon artificial stimulants, the drug addict is continually in the position of craving a "fix."

In this verse, David states that the person who trusts in God is never really afraid because his heart is "fixed" on the Lord. That's good news for us today, because in our society it seems that everyone has a dependency of some kind.

Materialistic people are dependent upon money for their happiness. Egocentric performing artists must have a continual supply of adulation and applause from their adoring fans. Authority figures are driven by a consuming hunger for power. Perverts have an insatiable appetite for "kinky" sex. Alcoholics lust after liquor to slake their never-ending thirst. Smokers crave nicotine constantly. Drug addicts are enslaved by their continual need of a "fix."

We Christians are dependent also. The difference is, we look to the Lord as our sole source of supply. Our dependence is on Him. This is not a mark of weakness; it is a mark of intelligence. Our reliance is upon the only absolutely dependable thing in the universe: the Lord Jesus Christ. Our heart is "fixed," because we trust in Him.

. . . when he (a thief) **is found, he must
restore sevenfold; he may have to give
up all the substance of his house.**

Proverbs 6:31 NKJ

This Bible verse tells us that a thief, when caught, has to make up to his victims seven times over what he has stolen from them — even if it means he has to empty his house to do so.

In John 10:10, the Lord Jesus Christ speaks of Satan, the original thief, who has come to steal, kill, and destroy. The Apostle John declares that Jesus was manifested to destroy the works of the devil. (1 John 3:8.) One of the works of Satan is stealing. He has been "found out" as mankind's greatest thief.

Jesus exposed the works of the enemy and showed him up for what he really is, the prince of thieves. Our text verse says that when a thief is discovered, he has to restore sevenfold what he has taken.

Some police departments, when apprehending a thief in possession of stolen goods, will ask property owners to make out a list of things missing so they can be returned to them.

Make out your list and present it to the Lord: "Lord, the enemy robbed me of peace of mind. I want it back sevenfold." "Lord, the enemy robbed me of health. I am requesting that health be returned to me, multiplied by seven." "Lord, the enemy robbed me of financial blessings. He has been found out as a thief, and I want my money back seven times over!"

The list could include anything you previously owned that has been stolen by the enemy. What you have lost to the devil, you can have restored to you sevenfold!

"Go therefore and make disciples of all the nations . . . ."
Matthew 28:19 NKJ

The original *King James Version* of this verse begins with this familiar injunction, **Go ye . . . .** This has probably been the one phrase which, more than any other, has inspired believers in every age to go forth to mission fields and proclaim sacrificially the Good News. "Go ye" has a certain ring to it. It is a commanding imperative. It motivates believers for a commitment to a life of unselfishness. "Go ye" moves people to disregard creature comforts and to boldly declare with the hymnist: "I'll go where you want me to go, dear Lord, O'er mountain or plain or sea; — I'll say what you want me to say, dear Lord, I'll be what you want me to be."

In addition to the challenging command "go ye," there is another option, an alternative reading of this verse. Besides "go ye," the opening phrase can be interpreted, "As you go . . . ."

All Christians are in motion. We are on a path leading to our eternal home. We are going through this life, led by the Spirit, and strengthened by the Word of God.

"As you go, make disciples of all nations." When you go to the post office, when you go to the store, when you go to work, to school, or to church. When you go on vacation. Whenever and wherever you go, be on the lookout for opportunities to share with others the Good News!

Not only go, but as you go — make disciples!

**"The Lord God has given Me the tongue
of the learned, that I should know how to
speak a word in season to him who is weary.
He awakens Me morning by morning, He
awakens My ear to hear as the learned."**

Isaiah 50:4 NKJ

Here Isaiah tells us how he received his messages from the Lord. Evidently, the prophet was just like any other normal human being. He seems to have kept the same laws of health that we do today. He ate and slept regularly. At morning time, when he was most rested and refreshed, most sensitive to spiritual responses, he would get a "nudge" from the Lord who would say to him: "Wake up, Isaiah, I have many things to tell you."

If you would like this to happen to you, then claim Proverbs 6:22 as a personal promise from the Lord to you: **. . . when you awake, they** (the words of God) **will speak with you.**

After the Lord had awakened Isaiah, He then opened his ears. Jesus often challenged His audiences: "He who has an ear, let him hear." Waking up is the first step. Hearing from the Lord is the next step. This is why a consistent plan of daily devotions is so vital to spiritual health.

As a result of awakening and listening to the Lord, Isaiah had the ability to say the right word to the right person in the right place at the right time. First his eyes were opened from sleep, then his ears were opened to God. Then was his mouth opened to speak sustaining and refreshing words to the languishing, weary followers of the Lord.

Eyes open, ears open, mouth open. That is a good sequence — for us as well as for Isaiah!

May 5

". . . go in and out and find pasture."
John 10:9 NKJ

"Go in and out." This is one of those balance verses. It tells us how to keep life on a normal, even keel by avoiding extremes.

Going in describes an aspect of life that is inward in scope. It refers to the practice of prayer, contemplation, meditation, fasting, solitude, and spending time alone with God. It stresses the need for a time of private fellowship with the Lord. Even though the Church is a community, an organism made up of many members, we are still individual believers with a personal relationship with our heavenly Father. We have a bond with the Lord that is best nurtured by daily communion with Him. When we go in, we often receive our marching orders and directions for that particular day.

Going out speaks of service to others. After we have gone in, sat at the feet of the Master, and received our directions, then we go out and communicate that truth to others by word and lifestyle. Going out is both a missionary journey and a mercy mission — an encouraging word accompanied and confirmed by a helping hand.

The two extremes are represented by: 1) those who have dedicated their lives to going in to God, and yet never, ever going out to a lost world, and 2) those who are so restless, nervous and hyperactive that they never cease "ministering" long enough to wait upon the Lord.

The ideal is a balance between the two: going in and going out — in that order. Go in *for* the message, go out *with* the message. To do so is to find pasture (rest and refreshment for the soul).

**. . . When you roam, they will lead you;
when you sleep, they will keep you; and
when you awake, they will speak with you.**

Proverbs 6:22 NKJ

Here Solomon is referring to commands, laws, precepts, and principles which his father and mother had taught him. He urges his son not to forsake or neglect them, but to keep them and value them highly. He assures his offspring that the Word of the Lord will lead him wherever he goes. It will stand guard over him as he sleeps. When he awakes in the morning, it will speak to him.

Years ago, I met people who told me they started the day with a scripture verse from the Lord. These dear friends were not mystical, ethereal, or metaphysically esoteric. They were down-to-earth, sensible, God-fearing, hard-working people devoted to serving the Lord and doing His will.

They shared with me how they had trained themselves to start the day with a "word from the Lord." This was the verse they used as a basis for their practice, for which they claimed three benefits: 1) their lives were serene, knowing they were guided by the Word, 2) their sleep was peaceful, knowing they were guarded by the Word, and 3) their waking was inspiring, knowing they would be given a word from the Lord for that day.

Tomorrow morning, instead of jumping out of bed and hitting the floor with a running start, why not wait 30 to 60 seconds and let the Lord give you a word of peace, joy or love. Proverbs 6:22 could read in this sequence: 1) *guided* by the Word, 2) *guarded* by the Word, 3) *goaded* by the Word. Try it; it works!

"Say to the righteous that it shall be well with them."
Isaiah 3:10 NKJ

When you were a child, didn't you like to hear stories which ended with the time-honored words, ". . . and they lived happily ever after"? Didn't you give a sigh of relief at the image of the hero and heroine finally having overcome all their obstacles and blissfully facing a wonderful new life together? Wasn't it satisfying to imagine the two of them — all their troubles behind them — happily riding off into the golden sunset?

This verse paints just such a bright, happy picture of the Lord and His Bride, the Church. It assures believers that they too will surmount the obstacles in their paths, overcome the difficulties which beset them on all sides, ride out the storms of life, and in the end find peace and joy and a marvelous new beginning. This verse expresses the Christian equivalent of "they lived happily ever after": **. . . it shall be well with them . . . .**

In the original Hebrew, the word translated **well** is *towb (tobe)* and can be defined as "good, gracious, joyful, prosperous, pleasant, precious." It denotes a state of general well-being. It is the word used to describe a person who has been ill but who has now regained his health. It is also used to speak of the state of an individual who has suffered financial reversal, but whose fortune has now been fully restored.

"Say to the righteous that it shall be well with them." Know that with God's intervention, things can always turn out the way they are supposed to. Don't expect the worst to happen, expect the best to take place. The Lord says that it shall be well with you. *Well.* Add this promising word to your vocabulary!

"I drew them with gentle cords, with bands of love . . . ."
Hosea 11:4 NKJ

This verse shows us the compassionate side of the Lord in His dealings with us mortals. He draws us with gentle cords and with bands of love. Like the great lover He is, He woos us closer and closer to Himself. He leads us, not by severity, but with tenderness.

When I was growing up in church, I can remember hearing all the horror stories of how God takes out His fierce anger upon all those who are in rebellion against Him. Such stories are uncomplimentary to the nature of our loving heavenly Father. They make it appear that God is out to "get" people. Too often, the Lord is portrayed as vindictive and relentless in His determination to reduce to dust and grind to powder anyone who dares to resist Him.

The point of these stories seems to be that when all resistance against the Lord is finally crushed, the agonizing soul totally surrendered and thoroughly chastened, then and only then will the Lord have mercy and turn away His anger. Growing up with such a concept of God did not help me to understand Him, His nature or His attributes. It was a welcome relief to me to discover in Scripture that it is the goodness of God — not His wrath — that leads men to repentance.

It is as though the Lord is saying to us through this verse: "You are getting closer to Me every day. Not because I am laying on you terrible diseases, horrible accidents, traumatic losses, debilitating financial reversals, and crushing personal failures. Rather, you are coming near to Me because I am drawing you with gentle cords and bands of love."

. . . **judge nothing before the time, until the Lord comes, who will both bring to light the hidden things of darkness and reveal the counsels of the hearts . . . .**

1 Corinthians 4:5 NKJ

You don't know what to do. You have to make a decision, but you know you need more information than you have at hand. This verse assures us that, regardless of the seeming urgency of the situation, it is best to wait until we are more knowledgeable than we are at present.

The usual interpretation of this verse by most scholars is that it concerns the *parousia (par-oo-see-ah)* or Second Coming, of the Lord Jesus Christ. When He returns, He will bring to light every hidden thing and rectify every injustice. "Wait till the Lord comes back to earth, and then we will see things in their true light."

This *is* the meaning of the verse. However, there are other events in our lives to which this verse can be applied equally as well. Besides the great *parousia* at the end of the age, Jesus comes to us in many ways: in salvation; in healing; in guidance; in deliverance from danger, crisis, and great need.

We could read this verse: "Do not take any hasty action; wait until the Lord has come onto the scene." There are subliminal factors hidden from your view. The Lord wants to bring to the level of your sight the things you need to know in order to make the right decision. You won't have to wait long. When you get the facts you need, you will know what action to take. Without those facts, you could do something you might later regret. When the Lord comes, you will be more knowledgeable and you will make the decision you can live with comfortably.

. . . He has put eternity in their hearts,
. . . no one can find out the work that
God does from beginning to end.

Ecclesiastes 3:11 NKJ

Here is a verse that explains why we go into all the world and preach the Gospel to every creature. God has put eternity in the heart of every person who has ever existed. Despite exterior appearance or attitude, deep down inside every living soul there is an inherent awareness of eternity. From the intellectual to the illiterate, all people have one thing in common — an intuitive inkling of the reality of life beyond death.

When He breathed into the first man the breath of life, the Creator placed within him an unextinguishable hope of another life beyond this present one. The presence of this deep-seated, universal hope is the basis of success of all evangelism, missionary outreach, and personal soulwinning. Knowing that God has already put into man's heart an awareness of eternity makes our job as witnesses not only possible but also much easier. We do not have to convict or convince anyone; all we have to do is to wisely and lovingly strike a responsive chord in the heart of each person with whom we share the Good News. When that chord is strummed, they *will* respond.

The second part of this verse says that although he is aware of eternity, man does not know the way to it. Our job as witnesses is simply to show people that way. We do that by telling them the Good News of Jesus, sharing with them God's plan for eternal life in Him.

Half of our job has already been done for us by the Lord when He placed within people the awareness of eternity. He has laid the foundation; we build His Church upon it — Jesus Christ being the chief cornerstone. (Eph. 2:20.)

**. . . on some have compassion,
. . . but others save with fear . . . .**
Jude 22,23 NKJ

This verse encourages sensitivity when dealing with unsaved people. Instead of strictly following a manual which purports to show how to witness to people, it is more preferable to let the Lord Himself adjust us and adapt us to each person's individual personality and disposition. Some people are farther along (in God's dealings with them) than others. We can be attuned to each person's capacity and spiritual receptivity. This verse tells us that there is a variety of ways people can be won to the Lord.

Instead of using the same technique with everyone, Jude tells us to use compassion with some and fear with others. Each case must be judged on its own merits. With sensitivity, we can adapt to each different situation. With some people I have had to be deadly serious, while with others I have been able to carry on a light conversation which even bordered on levity. Yet both approaches have produced good responses. What will "work" in one instance might be highly inappropriate or in poor taste in another.

Other translations of this verse suggest that we show compassion on those struggling with doubt, but fear with those who are arrogant, haughty, conceited, or rebellious. Proud, self-made people need breaking, broken people need mending. The Holy Spirit will show us each person's personal need and how to minister to that need.

Compassion or fear. They are both effective tools when used in the right way, at the right time, with the right person.

**. . . we do not know what we should pray
for as we ought, but the Spirit Himself
makes intercession for us . . . .**

Romans 8:26 NKJ

I have been in churches recently that were having "an hour of prayer" between 6 and 7 a.m. each day during the week. It has been quite encouraging attending gatherings around the world and finding sincere and conscientious working men, housewives, students, retired people, and church leaders all joining together to pray.

The comment is often heard from those not participating: "I don't know how to pray for a whole hour. I'm good for about five minutes of prayer and then my mind goes blank. What am I supposed to do the other 55 minutes besides let my mind wonder?" That is an honest question. It deserves an honest answer: this verse assures us of divine assistance.

This scripture acknowledges our limitations. We *don't* know how to pray as we ought. This is not a reproof or rebuke. It is a statement of fact. But this verse also tells us that the Holy Spirit helps us by making intercession for us.

If we will give Him the opportunity, the Holy Spirit will move inside us, prompting us to pray along certain avenues and for particular subjects. Given free rein, He will actually energize our prayer life, stirring us to fervent intercessory prayer. Jude calls this action "praying in the Holy Spirit." (Jude 20.)

When we allow the Spirit of God to pray *through* us, time is no problem.

He has made everything beautiful in its time . . . .
Ecclesiastes 3:11 NKJ

The original creation was so awesome, majestic, and beautiful that morning stars sang together and sons of God shouted for joy. (Job 38:7.) Flawless, perfect, and magnificent was that creation. God Himself examined it all and declared that is was "very good." (Gen. 1:31.)

But then an oppressive shadow came over this divine work of beauty. One of the head angels became self-willed and instigated an insurrection against the divine Creator. (Is. 14:12-15; Rev. 12:7-10.) As a result, creation became marred and disheveled.

As human beings, created by God, you and I are a miniature world, a microcosm of the original creation. We are a world of our own. Just as Genesis 1:1 tells of God's creating heaven and earth, so He also made us beautiful in our infancy. But under the influence of that fallen angel, like all of God's creation, we too became "damaged goods." When sin came into our lives, we became "emptiness and confusion." (Gen. 1:2.)

Salvation is a salvage work. Redemption is a restoration. Our Creator has intervened to give us beauty for ashes. Now that we are in Christ, we are no longer "damaged goods." His promise that He would send a Redeemer to beautify the meek with salvation has been fulfilled. (Ps. 149:4.) The defective has now been restored to its original pristine newness. (2 Cor. 5:17.)

Your God has made everything beautiful again. So . . . think beauty . . . talk beauty . . . walk beauty . . . believe beauty . . . . behave beauty . . . enjoy beauty! Because of Whose you are, you are beautiful!

**This is the day which the Lord hath made;
we will rejoice and be glad in it.**

Psalm 118:24

Which day is this verse talking about? Is it confined to one isolated day in human history?

The "day which the Lord hath made" began with the day of creation when morning stars sang together and all the sons of God shouted for joy. (Job 38:7.)

Another day of rejoicing occurred when Israel was led out of bondage in Egypt. David spoke of this day, saying of the Lord: . . . **he brought forth his people with joy, and his chosen with gladness** (Ps. 105:43).

That was a day of joyful deliverance. But it was not the only one. The day of Jesus' resurrection from the dead is also included in this verse. The anguish of the disciples, the sorrow of the women, the heavy gloom of the crucifixion — all this was replaced by the joy of an empty tomb: . . . **Then were the disciples glad, when they saw the** (risen) **Lord** (John 20:20).

Other days of rejoicing are the day of our own personal conversion, the day set aside each week to worship in the house of the Lord, and the day the Lord returns to claim His Bride, the Church.

Besides all these special days, let us remember that this age is often referred to as "the Gospel day." It is a day of God's making and its blessings are ours because our Lord has been placed as the head of the corner.

So therefore every day we live is the Lord's day and is a cause of joyous celebration!

**Let your speech always be with grace,
seasoned with salt, that you may know
how you ought to answer each one.**

Colossians 4:6 NKJ

There is a vast difference between salty speech and speech seasoned with salt. Salty speech is offensive, sarcastic, sharp, bitter, biting. Speech seasoned with salt is attractive, appetizing, flavorful, tasteful. It fulfills the very words of Jesus who urged His disciples to "have salt in yourselves." (Mark 9:50).

In sharing our faith with others, we need to be able to capture their interest and keep their attention. One way to do that is to make sure that our speech is well seasoned with salt. Just as salt adds appeal to food, so it adds appeal to our witness to others.

Salt enhances and enriches; it adds flavor to that which is dull, bland, and tasteless. Well seasoned speech adds flavor to the Bread of Life which we share with others to enhance and enrich their lives.

Salt is used as a preservative; it prevents corruption in meat. Likewise, "the meat of the Word" which we share with others can be kept pure and incorrupt when our speech is well seasoned with salt.

Salt produces thirst. Well salted speech can actually stimulate a thirst for the Water of Life.

In his New Testament commentary, Dean Alford states: "Salt as used by our Savior symbolizes the unction, freshness and vital briskness which characterizes the Holy's Spirit's presence and work in a man."

Without salt in our speech, our words will be insipid, banal, and uninspiring. Prayer makes the difference. A consistent life of daily prayer keeps the salt in our lives from losing its savor.

"The Lord called your name, Green Olive Tree, Lovely and of Good Fruit . . . ."
Jeremiah 11:16 NKJ

As a man, do people call you handsome? As a woman, are you considered beautiful? Well, according to this verse, this is the Lord's opinion of you! Maybe you don't see yourself as handsome or beautiful, but the Lord does. In this scripture, three unusual adjectives are used to describe you: **Green, Lovely,** and **Good.**

In the original Hebrew, this word translated **Green** is *ra'anan (rah-an-awn')*. It is defined as "new, prosperous, verdant, flourishing, thriving." It denotes great potential for growth. Thus, your spiritual name is "One Who Has a Great Capacity for Fruitfulness and Productivity in the Lord."

Lovely is from an original Hebrew word *yapheh (yah-feh')* meaning "beautiful, excellent, good, handsome." Bible grammarians note that this word is used primarily to describe men and women who are serving the Lord. Our heavenly Father has no "ugly ducklings" or "plain Janes." He has given His children beauty for ashes. Instead of downplaying yourself, verbally state that in God's eyes, you are handsome (male) or beautiful (female).

Of Good Fruit in Hebrew is a combination of *yapheh* and *to'ar (to'-ar)*, meaning "shape, form, figure, outline." Thus, you are "of beautiful form" or "of excellent figure." As a redeemed person, you have been translated from Satan's realm of little worth to Jesus' kingdom of great worth. He states that you are: 1) good looking, 2) thriving, and 3) in great shape!

May 17

> . . . get wisdom. And in all your
> getting get understanding.
>
> **Proverbs 4:7** NKJ

It is possible for a person to increase in knowledge and yet still be devoid of wisdom and understanding. The Bible assures us that knowledge will increase. We are living to see this prophecy fulfilled. Yet the crucial need of every person alive today is wisdom and understanding of God's dealings and purposes in his or her own individual life.

Pursuit of knowledge is a worthwhile endeavor. But it's not enough. An astronomer may know 100 times as much now about the solar system as his predecessors did a century ago, and still have no personal knowledge of the God who created both him and the solar system he so admires. According to Proverbs 9:10, knowledge of the Holy One produces understanding.

Understanding is important. Proverbs 3:19 (*NKJ*) tells us: **The Lord by wisdom founded the earth; by understanding He established the heavens.** Verse 13 says: **Happy is the man who finds wisdom, and the man who gains understanding.**

It is possible to increase knowledge and at the same time find wisdom and gain understanding of God's designs for us and our lives. Proverbs 2:2 (*NKJ*) exhorts us to incline our ears toward wisdom and to apply our hearts to understanding. Wisdom comes from an encounter with the Christ Who is the wisdom of God; understanding has to be sought and pursued. Success in life requires a solid edifice of wisdom and knowledge built upon a stable foundation of truth that cannot be swayed. That wisdom and knowledge can be acquired. It requires effort, but the reward is well worth the expense of time and energy.

For exaltation (promotion) **comes neither from the east nor from the west nor from the south.**

Psalm 75:6 NKJ

This verse came to me when I was working in a group of men doing road construction. The foreman told me I would never be promoted as long as he was in charge. He harbored hostility toward all Christians and bluntly stated, "We don't give promotions to milk drinkers, only beer drinkers." That left me out. When the promotion lists were posted on the bulletin board, my name was always notably absent.

I knew that I qualified for promotion, but I also knew that I was being purposely passed over because of the foreman's antagonism toward me. It was at this time that the Lord gave me this scripture as a promise.

If you will notice closely, the word *north* does not appear in this verse. As Christians, our promotion will ultimately come from the north. Look up the word *north* in a concordance and Bible commentary and you will find that it has a great deal of future import. (Is. 14:13.) When time runs out for this earth, you and I will say with the redeemed of all ages: "Our promotion came from the north from whence came our Savior to take us away!"

It was also during this time in my life that I received a visitation from the Lord. He imparted to me the ability to give "precious promises" to people by divine revelation. I didn't get a raise in salary, but I did receive a spiritual "boon." That should be no surprise: This verse tells us that our promotion always comes from the Lord!

May 19

**And that ye study to be quiet, and
to do your own business . . . .**
1 Thessalonians 4:11

Study is the key word here. Although not the same Greek word translated **study** in 2 Timothy 2:15 **(Study to shew thyself approved . . . .),** its meaning is similar. The *King James* translation of both words as *study* often leads people to think they refer to academic instruction or scholarship, when they actually have no connection at all with mental activity.

In this verse from Thessalonians, the word **study** is a compound Greek word whose definition reads: "to make an effort," "to be ambitious," "to make it a point of honor," "to exert oneself from a sense of love," and "to be motivated by an intense desire." In other words, Paul is saying here: *"Have no other ambition* than that of a quiet, industrious life."

The existing society in Paul's day was given to riots, community unrest, mob incitement and meddling in the affairs of others. Paul is telling the believers in Thessalonica to have a different goal. Their neighbors loved to be idle, to carry gossip and rumors, to stir up strife and contention. Some of this activity had crept into the church. Paul urges the believers to march to a different drumbeat: *"Make it your aim* to dwell safely and securely in a quiet, peaceful setting."

One version reads: "Keep yourself from all gathering of the idle, the restless, and the dissatisfied." To "study to be quiet" in the Greek suggests an all-out effort to maintain a lifestyle that is tranquil, serene, calm, and peaceful. It is worth it. The results can be lasting peace and harmony.

**Study to shew thyself approved unto God,
. . . rightly dividing the word of truth.**

2 Timothy 2:15

In the original Greek of this verse, the word translated **study** is *spoudazo (spoo-dad'-zo)* and has to do with quickness or promptness in one's efforts. One writer defines *spoudazo* as "to speed, make haste, and manifest oneself in diligence, earnestness, and zeal."

Originally, *spoude (spoo-day')* ("speed," dispatch, eagerness) and *spoudazo* were external words denoting quick movement in the interests of a person or cause. They implied carrying out a matter with speed and enthusiasm. Christianity applied these two words to an inner sphere of action, using them to relate to zealousness or eagerness, desire, or concern. The adjective form of these words could be defined as "busy, active, industrious." As a noun, they might be translated as "zeal, industry, effort, diligence or care (in contrast to laziness or sloth)."

For the person who is called to a career ministering the Word of God, this verse could be an incentive for an all-out, conscientious effort to please the Lord by prompt and eager obedience. Paul was saying: "The sooner you begin, the better. Don't delay. There's no time to lose. Get started, get on with it, get busy!"

Rightly dividing the word of truth is translated in *The Amplified Bible* as: 1) **. . . correctly analyzing . . .** 2) **accurately dividing —** 3) **rightly handling and** 4) **skilfully teaching — the Word of truth.** As Christian witnesses, we need to go "all out" in our eager, earnest efforts to learn to correctly handle the sword of the Spirit!

**A satisfied soul loathes the honeycomb, but
to a hungry soul every bitter thing is sweet.**

Proverbs 27:7 NKJ

Bitter herbs were part of the fare of the Jewish Passover. Ordinarily, they were an item that was considered unappetizing. Solomon is telling us here that if a person is hungry enough, even the bitterest of herbs tastes good to him.

Some missionaries have related this verse to overseas missions. They tell us that approximately ten percent of the world's population speak English, yet ninety percent of the world's Gospel ministers are concentrated in English-speaking areas. That leaves only ten percent of the world's preachers to minister to the needs of the ninety percent of the world's population which does not speak our language. That seems so disproportionate.

Some American cities have three Christian television stations, anywhere from five to ten Christian AM and FM radio stations, and three to ten Christian magazines for each believer's home. By contrast, we heard of a rural ministry in Haiti which had several ministers, but only one Bible. The ministers ended up breaking the Bible into smaller sections so each one could have at least a portion of the Holy Writ. How spoiled we Americans are!

The easiest way to avoid personal glut and saturation is to continuously pass on to others the good things the Lord is giving us. If we will keep the stream of revealed truth flowing out to the thirsty world, we will never become the satisfied, jaded soul who loathes the honeycomb. When the Lord blesses you with something good, pass it on!

**The Lord will arise . . . that He may
do His work, His awesome work, and
bring to pass His act, His unusual act.**

Isaiah 28:21 NKJ

This is a promise aimed right at those of us who are proper, precise, programmed people whose lives are well-planned and carefully ordered. The prophet is not faulting us for our efforts to prepare ourselves to face challenges, to figure solutions, or to work through all the obstacles that confront us in order to see our task completed. This verse is not an indictment against ambition, aggressive action, or well-developed plans for accomplishing what the faint-hearted would never even dare to attempt.

Rather, this scripture is an encouraging promise from the Lord that we will receive an answer to our prayers — on His terms and according to His timetable. It is an assurance that our heavenly Father is going to meet our needs — as He sees fit and when He sees fit. The answer may seem to be delayed, but when it does arrive it will be awesome and unusual.

Our Father is a God of infinite variety. He has a myriad of ways to respond to our petitions and requests. I did a preliminary lexical research study on this verse and came up with the following assurance: "Your prayer has been heard; the answer is on its way. It is a most unusual answer, and it is coming from the most unexpected source."

The most exciting part of the answer is the element of surprise! We all love a pleasant surprise — and this verse promises us just that!

Tell your children about it, let your children tell their children, and their children another generation.

Joel 1:3 NKJ

Here is a word covering four generations, from us to our children, to our grandchildren, to our great-grandchildren. It is a blessed word showing how the truth of God's Word can remain in a family for a long, long time.

In Deuteronomy 5:9, Moses stated that the sins of the fathers would be passed down through the family to the third and fourth generation. This verse in Joel is a positive assurance that the blessings of the Lord will also reach to the fourth generation.

It might be that very few people who read this devotional are great-grandparents. (My wife and I don't even come close.) However, despite our age or situation, there is a resident truth in Joel 1:3 for each of us. The truth is that our family is included in the promises of salvation. Again and again we read in Scripture the familiar phrase, "you and all your household." Truth resident in one's life has the potential for spreading through a family, and even through a whole family tree.

If you happen to be the only one in your family serving the Lord, rejoice. The Lord has chosen you to introduce salvation to all your loved ones. A little leaven leavens the whole lump. (Gal. 5:9.) You will live to see your entire family serving the Lord. It's just a matter of time!

**May I never boast except in the cross of our
Lord Jesus Christ, through which the world
has been crucified to me, and I to the world.**

Galatians 6:14 NIV

After having preached a milestone message in a
Southern California town, I was interviewed by a reporter
from a local newspaper who wrote an article claiming that
I had preached 2,500 times in ten years. That unsolicited
notoriety made me wonder: Would Paul have wanted his
ministry glorified that way? Surely not.

Some ministries publish how many countries they are
reaching, how many churches they have established, how
many missionaries they are supporting, how many busses
they run each Sunday, how many people their sanctuary
holds, how many different choirs they maintain, how many
converts they have won, and on and on.

I once knew of a ministry whose leaders boasted that
they had the largest staff of any church in the country. After
getting into financial difficulty, they called in a management
consultant team who advised them that they were greatly
overstaffed. To stay afloat, they were forced to let 200 church
workers go. Very soon afterwards, those same leaders were
once again boasting: this time that they had one of the
smallest staffs in one of America's largest churches!

In an age that is impressed with success, with bigness
and with numbers, this verse reminds us of where our
priorities really are. Part of the crucifixion to the world of
which Paul is speaking here is a death to the "numbers
game." It includes pride of grace, pride of race, pride of face,
and pride of place.

Do you think we Christians will ever learn that God is
not impressed with *our* achievements?

. . . "The beloved of the Lord shall
dwell in safety by Him . . . ."
Deuteronomy 33:12 NKJ

In a world full of evil, violence, and hatred, it is comforting to be promised *safety*. This word is vast and all-inclusive. Besides personal protection, it includes confidence, trust, security, and freedom from danger or fear. The original Hebrew word translated **safety** here is *betach (beh'-takh)*, meaning "a place of refuge." Thus this verse confidently assures us of our welfare and survival despite the vigors and uncertainties of this present unsettled age.

The beloved of the Lord includes all believers in Jesus Christ, especially those who are serving Him and doing His will. In Ephesians 1:6, the Apostle Paul declares that we believers are . . . **accepted in the beloved.** Acceptance by the Lord does not mean haughty exclusivism, privileged elitism, or entrance into a special inner circle. It simply makes possible that close personal relationship which exists between God and *all* those who will freely receive His gracious love.

The Bride of Christ is composed of redeemed people who are in many different stages of spiritual development. Regardless of our current level of spirituality, all of us make up the Beloved. As such, we are all promised safety, security, and confidence. We may think the Lord has "pets," "favorites," and "choice saints," those who have "an inside track" to His blessings or who enjoy a special "hot line" connection with Heaven. That is not so. We are all equal recipients of God's saving grace and therefore equal beneficiaries of His promised watchcare and safekeeping.

". . . I will even make a road in the wilderness . . . ."
Isaiah 43:19 NKJ

You can always tell the difference between negative people and positive people. The negative have a flair for defining the problem, while the positive have a gift for pointing out the solution.

It would be easy to be a "problem definer" these days; there's plenty of material available. Our environment reminds us constantly that "it's a jungle out there." Daily we are inundated by the media with reports of human depravity, crime, and violence. And, unfortunately, the vast majority of this information is factual and valid. We do indeed live in a "wilderness."

But if we are not careful, our conversation can easily become affected by all the negatives we see and hear about us. We can begin to major on the problem instead of the solution. It really isn't very edifying to continuously talk about the wilderness, especially when the Lord has told us through His prophet that He has provided a way through this "jungle."

Positive people talk more about the "road" than they do the wilderness. The Lord made that road. He has already walked it ahead of us. We know it is safe, reliable, and trustworthy. Others before us have safely traversed it from infancy to senior life. We are not consigned to groping through life trying to find our direction. The road itself is clear direction — the way to eternal and abundant life.

Take your choice: Define the problem, or declare the solution. Major in "wilderness talk" or "road talk." Talk over the woes, or talk up the way!

> . . . "But you stand here awhile, that I
> may announce to you the word of God."
> **1 Samuel 9:27** NKJ

How do we listen and move at the same time? How do we get direction and guidance while busily engaged in our regular activities? Is it possible to hear the voice of the Lord while we're talking to other people?

This verse illustrates how to go about getting guidance in the midst of "busy-ness." As they were going down to the outskirts of a certain city, the prophet Samuel said to King Saul, "Tell your companions to go on ahead of us and you will catch up to them in a minute. Right now I want you to stand here awhile and let me give you a word from the Lord."

I believe this is a good lesson on how to go about receiving needed guidance 1) on the run, 2) when right in the midst of activity, or 3) when surrounded by people. Busy people cannot always stop everything and go off on a retreat to get a further word of direction. But they can learn to take a minute to listen to the Lord, recognize His voice, and be attuned to receive divine guidance when needed most.

The key here is **awhile.** In the original Hebrew it indicates a short space of time: "Stand still just a moment." That's all it takes to get the message. Learning how to stop long enough to receive marching orders is a vital principle in learning to be led of the Spirit. On one hand, we don't want to pack our schedules so full of activities we can't stop and get direction. On the other hand, we don't want to withdraw into such an isolation that we never accomplish anything. The solution is learning to move and listen at the same time!

Then those who feared the Lord spoke to one another, and the Lord listened and heard them; so a book of remembrance was written before Him for those who fear the Lord and who meditate on His name.

Malachi 3:16 NKJ

This verse testifies to an unusual outpouring of God's grace and favor upon a group of people who served Him with their hearts in the midst of a society inclined to a rigid legal code. Three activities mentioned in this verse assure us of access to this same grace and favor: 1) speaking to one another, 2) fearing the Lord, and 3) meditating on His name.

1) *Speaking to one another.* Don't you enjoy the fellowship of other saints when the conversation is about the Lord and His doings? The Lord took notice of such conversation and rewarded it.

2) *Fearing the Lord.* This word **fear** does not refer to nervous compulsion or a guilty conscience, but to reverential awe, of being afraid of displeasing the Lord. According to Isaiah 11:2, this is one of the seven Spirits of God. It is available and desperately needed today. All we have to do is to pray and we as individuals, a family, or a church will receive this reverent Spirit.

3) *Meditating on the name of the Lord.* The powerful, majestic, glorious name of God became the object of these people's meditation.

Because they did these things, the Lord wrote a book of eternal remembrance for His people. He will do the same for us: we can make history by applying this verse.

" '. . . the battle is not yours, but God's.' "
2 Chronicles 20:15 NKJ

We are soldiers in a fight to the finish. The final outcome of that battle has already been determined. The Lord God omnipotent reigns. (Rev. 19:6.) He is coming with ten thousands of His saints to establish His kingdom on this earth. (Jude 14.) The government shall be upon His shoulder, and of His kingdom there shall be no end. (Is. 9:6.) We shall reign with Him forever and ever. (Rev. 22:5.)

Ours is a warfare in which the victory has already been announced ahead of time, but we do have individual skirmishes. We have our own private battles with pride, lust, anger, fear, and a host of other opponents. Because He has overcome the flesh, the world, and the devil, the Lord Jesus assures us that we too can overcome. (Rev. 12:11.) His example motivates us to believe for total victory.

The battle is the Lord's; it is His truth against Satan's lie, His light versus the enemy's darkness. This warfare pits health against sickness, faith against fear, prosperity against poverty, and godliness against iniquity. We fight in this war, but it is the Lord Who gives the victory. At times it may seem that we Christians are outnumbered and even outmatched, but we can take courage and inspiration from the knowledge that we are on the side of ultimate triumph.

With the Lord on our side, we can say: "The battle is the Lord's; the victory is the Lord's!" Blessed assurance!

**. . . For He Himself has said, "I will
never leave you nor forsake you."**
Hebrews 13:5 NKJ

This is a quotation from three Old Testament references: Deuteronomy 31:6 and 31:8 and Joshua 1:5. The writer of Hebrews simply updates these promises and gives them a New Testament setting. The Lord Jesus is now seated on the throne of God and is waiting for the signal from His Father to descend into the earth's atmosphere to be joined together physically with His waiting Church. (1 Thess. 4:16,17.)

While we who look for His appearing are going through our preparation time in anticipation of His return, we can be comforted in knowing that He has promised to be with us at all times. He has assured us that wherever two or three are gathered together in His name, there He is in their midst. (Matt. 18:20.)

Besides His presence with us as a corporate body, He has sent the Holy Spirit to indwell our individual bodies. The Holy Ghost always magnifies Jesus. Thus the spirit of prophecy (words given by the Holy Spirit to individual believers) becomes the very testimony (revelation) of Jesus Himself.

So in the Person of the Holy Spirit, Jesus resides continually in our tabernacles of stone (our churches) as well as in our tabernacles of clay (our bodies). Even though Jesus is in heaven with His Father, He has emphatically pronounced His abiding presence with us. One Greek scholar has translated Hebrews 13:5 with five negatives: "I will never, never, never, never [under no circumstances, be they ever so difficult] desert you." I believe this is a powerful assurance for all of us.

May 31

Let God arise, let His enemies be scattered . . . .
Psalm 68:1 NKJ

Scattering the enemy is God's plan for diffusing the malignant forces that come against the believer. Scattering the enemy breaks up his power base so that his intensity is fragmented and his designs thwarted.

When God arises in our behalf, two things happen: 1) We receive a deliverance wrought by divine intervention. God comes to our rescue and lifts us out of our adversity; 2) The enemy that posed a united threat to our progress becomes splintered and pulverized. The Lord's word of deliverance becomes a hammer to break the rock in pieces. (Jer. 23:29.) The enemy comes against us one way, but when God arises to confront him, he flees before us seven ways. (Deut. 28:7.)

Solomon tells us that a wise king scatters the wicked. (Prov. 20:26.) When you see organized opposition, collective hostility, and the enemy marshalling his forces to come against the cause of righteousness, know that God will step in and bring to naught the devices of the adversary.

Oh, blessed comfort, knowing that the Lord is looking out for our protection and preservation! Let God arise, and let His enemies be scattered. Our enemy is also His enemy. Our battles become His battles. Gloriously, His victory becomes our victory.

If anyone speaks, let him speak
as the oracles of God . . . .
1 Peter 4:11 NKJ

The short word! That's what *oracles* means. In the original Greek, *logion (log'-ee-on)* is defined as "a brief, terse, succinct, concise, or short utterance."

It is one thing to have an answer, it is another thing to be able to give that answer without turning it into a long, drawn-out, elaborate discourse. If anyone speaks, let him speak as the *logion* of God, as one who delivers a direct and honest word.

Thayer's Greek-English lexicon tells us that all prophecies in New Testament times were brief (and to the point). In this same epistle, Peter urges us to always be ready to give an answer for the hope that is in us as believers. That answer does not need to be an hour-long dissertation. It should be the *logion* of God, a short, concise word.

I remember with painful amusement a question and answer session I participated in as a guest on CBN's 700 Club. At that time, Israel had just invaded Lebanon and the whole world was carefully watching the outcome. A lady in the studio audience asked me point blank, "Will this incident speed up the coming of the Lord?" As I look back upon the question, I realize that I could have answered it with a simple yes or no. Just that easy! Instead, I stammered around for three or four minutes and never did answer the lady's question. In that situation I certainly was not an oracle.

Let's be oracles. Let's speak as the *logion* of God. Let's make our words brief and to the point!

". . . give us a measure of revival in our bondage."
Ezra 9:8 NKJ

Bondage, in this verse, does not refer to the bondage of sin. We believers have been delivered from that. It does not refer to the bondage of sickness or infirmity. We have also been set free from all that. This does not even refer to trying to live in the Spirit while resisting the cravings of the old Adamic nature within us — though that is a legitimate concern.

Here Ezra is asking the Lord for a measure of revival in the bondage of his *circumstances*. He is surrounded by people given over to idolatry. Seeing the gross practices of sensual people will always adversely affect those who seek to walk in the Spirit.

Bondage exists when a Spirit-minded believer has to work in an office filled with earthly-minded people who have no relish for spiritual things. Bondage exists when a Christian student finds himself surrounded by non-believers who make it clear that they neither share nor appreciate his interest in the things of God. Bondage exists when a believer's whole neighborhood majors on partying rather than on praying, when even his church is caught up in trivial social functions rather than in ministering to vital, pressing needs.

Living in this world of disbelief and unconcern can tend to stifle or suffocate us. The Lord wants to revive us so we can walk in freedom and love. If you will read the next verse (Ezra 9:9), you will see that the Lord did revive His people. He will do the same for us today!

. . . "I am the Lord your God, who
teaches you to profit . . . ."
Isaiah 48:17 NKJ

Profiting is more than making money. It can include financial increase, but it has a much more blessed scope than just material things. The Hebrew word translated **profit** here is *ya'al (yaw-al')*. It has to do with climbing or ascending, excelling, gaining ground, rising above circumstances, reaching the top or summit. *Ya'al* is also the Hebrew word for the ibex or wild goat which was so named because of his climbing ability.

Ya'al is used negatively throughout Scriptures to refer to people who put value on the wrong pursuits. Israel is often told by God that idols will not profit them. Trusting in the military might of Egypt is unprofitable; rather, they should trust in the Lord their God. Solomon tells us that **riches profit not in the day of wrath . . . .** (Prov. 11:4). We are to gain riches during the Gospel days and disperse them before the coming of the Lord. Our riches can be utilized for evangelism and missionary outreach now while producing eternal rewards.

One generous pastor, well known for giving away everything yet still prospering, has said: "Everything that comes into my life is flowing out to others. I don't want $20 in my wallet when the Second Coming takes place; I don't want to leave anything to the Antichrist!"

Satan is forever trying to demean, discourage and destroy us. The Lord has promised to teach us to profit, to raise our levels, to improve the quality of our lives, to help us to ascend in life. Satan wants us to go downhill, the Lord is taking us up to higher ground!

June 4

"And I will rebuke the devourer for your sakes . . . ."
Malachi 3:11 NKJ

The **devourer** needs to be defined. The Hebrew word *akal (aw-kal')* means "to eat, consume or burn up." It was used by Bible writers to define the actions of drought, famine, war, pestilence, and plague. To "rebuke the devourer" is to check, curb, and deter anything that consumes time, energy, or cash-flow.

In this verse the Lord promises to put a stop-gap on that which consumes our time. How many times have you started out a day with a plan for getting things done, only to look back at the end of the day and realize that your time had gotten away from you? The Lord has promised to rebuke the devourer of time.

The same promise applies to energy. During the average eight-hour workday, we expect to achieve a stated number of goals, to complete so many assigned tasks, to produce a certain predetermined amount of output for our efforts. It is always disconcerting to look back at the end of the day and compare how much we intended to get done with how little we actually accomplished. The Lord has promised to rebuke the devourer of energy.

This promise also applies to money. You buy tires, and they wear out too soon. You buy shoes, and they do not last. You buy groceries, and run out before the week is over. You spend money, yet have nothing to show for it. God has promised to rebuke the devourer of finances.

With God's blessings, you and I can get 60 minutes of time out of every hour, eight hours of productivity out of each working day, and a hundred pennies of value out of every dollar spent. What a blessing!

**". . . I will . . . open for you the windows of
heaven and pour out for you such blessing that
there will not be room enough to receive it . . . ."**
Malachi 3:10 NKJ

Windows **of heaven!** What a beautiful, illustrious,
picturesque word! Other translators use the words "sluices,"
"floodgates," or "apertures." In any case, this is a promise
of a deluge of blessings coming upon those who lead lives
marked by generosity.

The windows of heaven are mentioned in two other
places in the Bible: one is negative and the other positive.
In 2 Kings 7:2 and 7:19, Elisha predicts that the famine is
over and that the price of food will soon be incredibly
reduced. The king's squire responds in disbelief, "If the Lord
opened windows in heaven, this thing might be." Elisha's
reply is: "You will see it, but never partake of it." When the
news of the miraculous turn-around hits the streets, the
famished people rush out of the city to gather up the much-
needed supplies. In their haste, they run over and acciden-
tally trample to death the skeptical squire — just as the
prophet had foretold.

The windows of heaven are also mentioned in Noah's
day when the Lord opened the skies and deluged the earth
with rain for forty days. (Gen. 7:11; 8:2.)

Thus the windows of heaven are mentioned three times
in Scripture with three different applications: 1) a deluge
of rain (we can compare this to revival or spiritual renewal),
2) a miraculous supply following a great famine, and 3) an
overflowing provision of blessings in the lives of believers.
What a promise!

. . . a threefold cord is not quickly broken.
Ecclesiastes 4:12

One strand of cord can be easily severed. Two strands of cord can be stretched and pulled until they split. But a threefold cord is not easily broken.

The New American Standard Bible reads: **. . . A cord of three strands is not quickly torn apart.** Scripture never tells us exactly what these three strands symbolize. In a case like this, there is usually much conjecture. Listed below are several suggestions for what the threefold cord represents:

1. HAM, SHEM, AND JAPHETH. *Family ties.* Man had a serious family rupture from the time of Adam to Noah. With his three sons to help him and each other, Noah (mankind) had a better chance of survival.

2. ABRAHAM, ISAAC, AND JACOB. *Covenant relationship.* Naming these three and claiming the individual blessings upon them was like having a threefold benefit.

3. THE LAW, THE PROPHETS, AND THE WRITINGS. *Three divisions of the Old Testament.* These three made up truth as revealed to Israel.

4. FATHER, SON, AND HOLY GHOST. *Threefold cord of deity.* Nothing can sever or mar the unity of God.

5. SPIRIT, SOUL AND BODY. *Triune nature of redeemed man.* All three must be integrated and functioning in harmony in order for the believer to be at his best.

6. MAN, WIFE, AND CHILD. *Basic family unit.* It has been proven that a child cements a marriage more than anything else.

7. (YOUR INTERPRETATION.) I have left this one blank so you can send me your suggestions. I would be interested in *your* response!

**. . . I will settle you after your old estates, and will
do better unto you than at your beginnings . . . .**
Ezekiel 36:11

Whoever heard of anyone breaking down and then
coming back better than ever? Our cynical world says
sarcastically: "One strike, and you're out!"; "Opportunity
only knocks once; if you missed it, too bad"; "If you've had
a divorce, or a stroke, or gone bankrupt, you'll never recover
completely, you'll never be the same again"; "Once you're
down, you've had it, you may as well give up!"

That is not the Lord's report. Here He is addressing a
group of dispossessed people taken captive 550 miles to the
northeast of their homeland. They were uprooted and
removed from every kind of living they had ever known.
The Lord is promising them a release, a return, a recovery,
and a restoration:

"I will bring you back to where you were before your
trouble started. I will do better to you than at your begin-
ning. You will not only make a comeback, you will be better
than ever."

As soon as you and I became believers in the Lord Jesus
Christ, a whole world of promises opened up to us. All these
reassuring promises tell us to expect things to get better, that
our life can be improved upon. The world cannot promise
this to us, but the Lord can and does.

Perhaps you feel as if you have lost everything, that it's
too late for you. If so, I have good news; the Lord is about
to do great things for you!

June 8

. . . "In quietness and confidence
shall be your strength."
Isaiah 30:15 NKJ

This verse assures us of quietness and confidence — in that order. Find quietness, and confidence will follow after it as a matter of course.

These two are twins — two friends to go with us on our pilgrim's journey. As the psalmist David declares in Psalm 23 that goodness and mercy shall follow him all the days of his life, so this verse proclaims that we can expect quietness and confidence to accompany us as we travel the road of life.

Quietness is not passivity, fatalism, or a state of detachment. Quietness is not resignation to a painful situation, a sort of "why try?" mindset or outlook. Quietness is a total absence of noisy distraction, tumultuous turmoil, of frantic, hectic pressure. It is God's gift of peace given right in the midst of labor and activity. Quietness is not an absence of problems or trials, it is an undisturbed calm that says in the midst of difficulty and tribulation, "It's all right; God is in control." Such calmness produces confidence.

Confidence is translated elsewhere as assurance and boldness. In the midst of quietness, confidence surfaces and emerges as a potent force.

The Lord gives quietness to the seeking, praying soul. The end result is confidence. Girded about with these two spiritual powers, we can proceed with a new strength and determination to finish the task we have been called to accomplish.

". . . to give them beauty for ashes . . . ."
Isaiah 61:3 NKJ

Ashes are the only thing left when dreams go up in smoke.

A young woman enters marriage full of high hope and a wonderful dream. The marriage sours, the hope is shattered, the dream is gone; she is left looking at a pile of ashes.

A young man goes into business with aspirations of greatness. Errors in judgment, changing tides, wrong decisions, and he goes bankrupt. Ashes!

Good health, good friendships, good plans for the future can all go up in flames overnight leaving nothing but the blackened ashes of disappointment, disillusionment, and despair.

This observation may seem gloomy and depressing, but it doesn't have to be. There is an answer. Only the Lord can turn ashes into a thing of beauty. He can take any broken situation, mend it, and make it into an object of art, a thing of beauty, a joy forever.

If you are "burnt out," don't wallow in the ashes of self-pity. Let the Lord take over your life from here on. See what He will do with it. His creativity will surprise you!

Faced with ashes, we humans tend to finalize by concluding: "Well, that's it; it's all over. There's nothing left." In this verse, the Lord steps in and literally makes something out of nothing. He has the ability to take our worst losses and turn them into powerful displays of divine beauty!

. . . You shall surround me with songs of deliverance.

Psalm 32:7 NKJ

A lady in Pasadena, California, was awakened out of a sound sleep by this word from the Lord: "Pray for Dick Mills; his life is in danger." For twenty minutes she prayed in the Spirit, interceding for me. As she prayed she began to sing confidently, "There is power, power, wonder working power, in the blood of the Lamb." She later told me of the incident, relating how peace came over her at the time the song came to her. She instinctively knew then that the danger had passed.

At precisely the same time this intercession was taking place, I was in real danger of being shot and killed by a deranged killer as I was helping one of his accomplices escape from him. In a mission meeting some time before, I had helped Jolie come back to the Lord from a backslidden condition. His prison mate heard about it, and set out for revenge. At the time of the prayer, he was following us down the street threatening our lives. His threats were not idle ones, since Jolie told me that he had seen him kill five different men.

I don't understand all of God's dealings. While I was standing there on the sidewalk watching this man come toward Jolie and me, the same Holy Spirit moving on the intercessor in Pasadena began to plant the same song in my spirit. On the outside, I was shaking, but on the inside I was singing, "There's power in the blood." Same song, same time.

Suddenly, Jolie said, "Uh-oh, here he comes! We are as good as dead." That really didn't seem to me the best time for a song service, but I couldn't turn it off. As I sang, we walked right past the killer unnoticed and escaped unharmed.

Truly we were surrounded by a song of deliverance!

**"I sent you to reap that for which you
have not labored; others have labored,
and you have entered into their labors."**

John 4:38 NKJ

There are sowers and there are reapers. Preliminary work and preparation is often done by those who never get to see the result of their labors. Those who do the planting have to believe that their contribution is going to terminate in a good harvest, whether they get to experience the joy of gathering that harvest or not.

Here, however, the emphasis is reversed. The Lord Jesus tells His disciples that they are going to reap a harvest planted by someone who preceded them. He could be referring to Old Testament workers, to John the forerunner, or to Himself.

Our Lord is saying to His disciples: "I am sending you in to reap a harvest. Others ahead of you have done all the preliminary preparation. The ground work has been taken care of. All you have to do is reap the benefits of their labor."

Prophetically speaking, this verse could apply to you and me. Nearly two thousand years of planting, sowing, irrigating, weeding, hoeing, and cultivating have gone into the Gospel ministry. It is now harvesttime, time to reap all the benefits and blessings that go with the worldwide harvest of souls for the kingdom. The early evangelists, intercessors, and soulwinners have done their part. Now it's our turn. Our part is to enter their labors and gather in the harvest they have made possible. The fields are white unto harvest. The time is now!

"Little by little I will drive them out from before you,
until you have increased, and you inherit the land."

Exodus 23:30 NKJ

In this verse the Lord is assuring Israel that the
dispossession of Canaan's inhabitants will not occur all at
once, but that it will take place. In verses 28 and 29 He
explains that if these people were all driven out at once, they
would leave behind a new problem: wild, marauding
animals would multiply and become a menace. Instead, the
Lord promises to remove the inhabitants little by little as the
Israelites increase enough to handle the occupation of their
inheritance.

What a message to us! God has to build us up to handle
promotion. We need to be groomed for success. Nobody
starts at the top. You don't come out of a high school business
class and begin your career as vice-president of the bank.
No one goes directly from seminary to the bishop's chair
in one jump.

Little by little can be likened to the rings of a tree. It
takes one whole year to complete that ring. By some people's
standards, that is "too slow." But each year that goes by, each
ring that is completed, the roots of that tree go down farther
into the ground, the branches reach higher into the sky, and
the tree gains additional size and strength to withstand the
storms of life which assail it.

Do you think we believers will ever learn that God's
timing is wisest for us?

**. . . the love of God has been poured out in
our hearts by the Holy Spirit who was given to us.**

Romans 5:5 NKJ

Here is a promise of an abundance of *agape* love, the
God-like love which gives expecting nothing in return. This
promise has to do with loving the unlovely, those who
cannot, or will not, return that love. This verse means a great
deal to missionaries who give up creature comforts and
personal ease among their own people in order to take the
Gospel message to a foreign people far away who many
times neither desire nor appreciate such personal sacrifice
on their behalf.

"Yankee, go home!" is not just a political slogan. Often
it is the "buzz word" American missionaries of all denomina-
tions and churches hear from hostile nationals who
misunderstand and resent their "intrusion" into their every-
day lives.

What would prompt a person to leave familiar and
pleasant surroundings and go hundreds, even thousands,
of miles away to invest his life in a strange, uncomfortable
and often dangerous environment? Especially when that
sacrifice seems to be neither recognized nor rewarded? Those
missionaries I talk to share how the *agape* love of God so
overwhelmed them that they had no other choice but to
respond to the call to the mission field. That love so
motivated them that they would only complain if they did
not get to go.

God's love is the greatest power in the universe. Once
people see and recognize the reality of that love
demonstrated before them, their response changes from
"Yankee, go home!" to "Friend, please stay and tell us more
about this Jesus!" That makes it all worthwhile!

June 14

Who forgives all your iniquities,
who heals all your diseases.

Psalm 103:3 NKJ

Salvation and healing are inseparable. The same Lord who forgives our sins, heals our diseases. In both the Old Testament and the New Testament, the word *salvation* is all-inclusive, including within its meaning forgiveness, reconciliation, deliverance, healing, safety, rescue, setting at liberty.

When Israel left Egypt, the sacrificial lamb slaughtered before their departure served two purposes. The blood of the lamb sprinkled on the doorposts protected the people from the judgment of sin that came that passover night. The flesh of the lamb was eaten to provide sustenance and strength for the journey ahead. The physical benefits were so great that Psalm 105:37 (*NKJ*) states of God's people: **. . . there was none feeble among His tribes.** One lamb covered both spiritual and physical needs.

Jesus went about forgiving sins and healing the sick. (Acts 10:38.) He told the twelve to do the same. He told the seventy to do the same. He could have told the five hundred to do the same. Everyone called to preach the Gospel of forgiveness for sin is also told to heal the sick. The two are inseparable.

Every time we take Communion, we are reminded of man's two areas of need: spiritual health and physical health. The cup reminds us that the blood of Jesus takes away all our sins. The wafer, or broken bread, reminds us that with His stripes we are healed. Salvation and healing come to us through the life and death of Jesus Christ. You can claim them both!

. . . as long as he sought the Lord,
God made him prosper.
2 Chronicles 26:5 NKJ

All the scriptural promises of prosperity are conditional. Our hearts' response to the Lord and our desire to seek Him and to please Him assure us of His blessings of prosperity.

This verse reveals to us that King Uzziah of Judah prospered as long as he sought the Lord. The same principle applies to you and me today. By our attitude and actions, we predetermine to what extent — and for how long — the promises of prosperity are fulfilled in our lives. A lifetime of dedicated pursuit of the Lord and His righteousness and ways equals a lifetime of gifts bestowed on us by a benevolent Divine Providence.

The prophetic promise of 2 Chronicles 15:2 is addressed to you and me today just as much as it was to King Asa of Judah in ancient times: . . . **"The Lord is with you while you are with Him. If you seek Him, He will be found by you; but if you forsake Him, He will forsake you"** (*NKJ*). As long as the king sought the Lord, he prospered. This word *prospered* has to do with advancement, promotion, gaining ground, increasing resources.

We do not seek or serve the Lord for mercenary reasons; we do so because as Creator of heaven and earth He is worthy of all our spiritual pursuit and devotion. But it is a joy to know that as we seek our heavenly Father with ardent spiritual intensity, He blesses us with all spiritual blessings. The additional benefits include physical health and financial prosperity. As children of the King, let's stop living beneath our station in life! Let's claim our inheritance, our glorious privileges! Let's seek the Lord!

You, O God, sent a plentiful rain, whereby You confirmed Your inheritance, when it was weary.

Psalm 68:9 NKJ

Years ago a scholar coined a phrase to describe the state of 20th-century saints who have grown fatigued in the march from earth to heaven. The expression he used was "pre-millennial weariness." Not a pre-millennial rapture, but a state of fatigue which settles in on those who have labored long and hard for a lifetime and yet who must still go on waiting for the Lord to return.

This verse recalls marching Israel spending forty years on their journey to the Promised Land. The trip seemed interminable. Weary, worn, beset with problems and difficulties, they fretted with impatience, questioned their leadership, complained about their surroundings. Morale was low and even Moses could not really answer their constant question, "How much longer?"

It was at this moment of low ebb that the Lord sent a deluge of rain. One translator calls it "a rain of free gifts." That's all it took to revive and refresh the souls of the weary pilgrims.

The same principle applies to us today. The church age has lasted nearly 2000 years now. Weary hearts are asking, "How much longer?" The Lord's answer is an invigorating rain of Holy Spirit blessings which the book of Acts calls "rain from heaven and fruitful seasons." The hymnist spoke for us as he cried out for such "seasons refreshing." With that refreshing, we will be able to make the rest of the journey in flying colors and full strength.

Lord, grant not just "showers of blessings," but send "a plentiful rain"!

. . . . established in the present truth.

2 Peter 1:12 NKJ

There seems to be a concern in some quarters of the Church today about the words **present truth.** This is an unnecessary fear, one which must be dealt with lest it deprive us of God's revelation knowledge for our time.

It seems that those who are resistant to the use of the expression "present truth" object to it on the grounds that it suggests acceptance of "a new gospel not founded on the Bible." This is a needless anxiety. There is no real danger in the Christian Church that the Bible will ever be replaced by a "revelation" given to some modern-day guru or cult leader.

The problem is a misunderstanding of the words **present truth.** In the original Greek, this was one word, *pareimi (par-i-mee),* meaning "the truth at hand" or "the truth for the time being." In each period of revival, a new *aspect* of well-established *scriptural* truth has come to the forefront and received a Spirit-inspired focus and emphasis: In Luther's day it was "justification by faith"; in Wesley's age it was "today is the day of salvation"; during the Holiness revival period it was "without holiness no man shall see God." The Pentecostal's "present truth" is "Jesus Christ, the same yesterday, today, and forever."

" ' "**He who has an ear, let him hear what the Spirit** *says* **to the churches**" ' " (Rev. 3:22 *NKJ*). God's Word is forever settled in heaven and will never be replaced. The Holy Spirit, however, has something to say to this age, just as He does to every age. He delivers that message by *speaking* to believers. Be listening for God's eternal, everlasting, "*present* truth"!

June 18

While Peter was still speaking these words, the Holy Spirit fell upon all those who heard the word.

Acts 10:44 NKJ

Here we see portrayed a unique human-divine drama, a picture of natural and supernatural teamwork. Peter is a human being, using human vocal chords, phrasing human sentences, speaking words in human language to human listeners who understood him on human terms. That is all natural.

The supernatural part is that while Peter was thus functioning at the earthly, human level, the Holy Spirit fell on all the listeners, working within their hearts what only Spirit can accomplish. The result of this human-divine teamwork was a whole household of people converted to Christ and instantly filled with the Spirit of God.

Peter spoke **words** (plural) externally, and the Holy Spirit "co-operated" or "co-labored" with him by causing the crowd to hear **the word** (singular) internally. The power was not in Peter himself or even in his words, but in the Spirit who translated words into Word! Someone has put it this way: "Peter was not giving a book review, a weather report, crime statistics, or a political opinion. He was proclaiming God's Word." That Word is the vehicle the Lord blesses, the channel through which He moves and acts.

As Christians, you and I can expect the same positive response Peter received — if we do what Peter says he always did: preach the Gospel *with the Holy Ghost sent down from heaven.* (1 Pet. 1:12.) Let's proclaim the Word of God, and trust Him to work with us by His Spirit to produce miraculous results!

". . . I free you this day from the chains that were on your hand . . ."

Jeremiah 40:4 NKJ

Free at last! What a word of final deliverance this is. Not only does the Lord promise through the prophet liberation and removal of all chains, He also assures that those chains will never be put back on: **. . . the Egyptians whom you see today, you shall see again no more forever** (Ex. 14:13,14). In other words: "The problems you have been facing up to now, you will never have to face again forever." To one who has been bound in chains, that is good news!

I had parked the car and was taking a shortcut through an alley to the church I was attending. I saw a man sitting there in the darkness. He was dejected and miserable. I recogized him as a person I had previously known. When I asked him what he was doing there in that dismal place, he showed me the needle marks in his arm.

An expensive heroin habit had done its job well, transforming a respected, productive human being into a derelict of society who could not function without a daily "fix." What had once been a free man was now a prisoner of drugs. Imagine the joy which was mine to be able to share with this one bound in darkness that Jesus breaks every chain, forever!

With the Lord in our hearts and lives, you and I never have to give up. No situation is impossible with Him on our side. This verse was given to let us know that our freedom has been purchased. Because the Deliverer has come, we can be *free at last*!

**And the Lord restored Job's losses . . . . Indeed,
the Lord gave Job twice as much as he had before.**

Job 42:10 NKJ

What a thrilling conclusion to the book of Job! Imagine
forty-one chapters describing the life of a man sorely tested
and severely tried by all kinds of discouraging circumstances.
The Bible tells us that Job emerged from his adversity with
a double portion of blessings. Only the Lord can truly end
a story with the promise of living "happily ever after." The
world has no power to assure anyone that his life story will
conclude on a happy note.

As a child, I was brought up on the Prince Charming
story in which the hero overcomes all obstacles and defeats
a fierce dragon as he battles his way to the enchanted castle
to rescue Sleeping Beauty from a wicked curse. At the end,
the two lovers ride off into the sunset bathed in "hearts and
flowers." Solid romance!

But the story usually doesn't come out that way
anymore. Today's generation is supposed to demand a more
"realistic" approach, so the writer might have a terrorist
group plant a bomb under Beauty's bed to blow them both
to kingdom come! Another writer might suggest filling the
moat with crocodiles so Prince Charming gets discouraged,
gives up, and goes home to become a hairdresser! Madison
Avenue would have Beauty wake up accusing the Prince of
having "ring around the collar!"

Despite society's negative viewpoint, for the Christian,
life doesn't have to end on a "downbeat." Everything in the
Bible points to an ending that is "upswing." Job ends up with
twice the blessings he started out with. *That's* God's intended
plan for us!

**". . . for the children have come to birth,
but there is no strength to bring them forth."**
Isaiah 37:3 NKJ

This is a call for intercessors. The Church goes through its prenatal time of preparation for its converts. Before people can be born again, the Church has its periods of intercessory travail. Prayer, fasting, petition, and supplication are all necessary ingredients for additions to the Christian family. Isaiah's lament is due to a languishing nation. The children were ready to be born, but the spiritual vitality was so low there was not strength enough to bring forth.

Over 350,000 churches exist in the United States. Someone has estimated that one half of them do not add even one convert a year. Spiritual sluggishness and lack of spiritual strength keeps the births from happening.

Healthy women have healthy babies. Vigorous women have vigorous babies. Lively women have lively babies. Healthy, vigorous lively churches will produce born-again babies in Christ who have a chance of surviving. Only a vigorous ministry of prayer for an individual or a church can turn spiritual listlessness to spiritual vitality. It is in such a setting that new births will occur.

. . after the fire a still small voice.
1 Kings 19:12 NKJ

The message of this verse is "personality adjustment." In this situation, God was changing a man. In his early days, Elijah's life was stormy. He could recognize and relate to wind, earthquake, and fire. His whole prophetic career was characterized by these three qualities.

God was mellowing Elijah. By a set of circumstances and the Lord's personal dealings, the prophet ended up on the same mountain where Moses had received the Jewish law. The cave he found himself in could have been the same "cleft of the rock" in which the Lord hid Moses when His glory passed by and Moses was allowed to view God's back. (Ex. 33:20-23.)

In Moses' case, as the Lord passed by him, there was wind, earthquake, and fire. It was in this tumultuous setting that he was given the Ten Commandments. Now we read that in this same location many years later Elijah was also met by the Lord. As in Moses' case, there was wind, earthquake, and fire. But God was not in any of these violent things. Instead, the Lord came in the form of "a still small voice" — a soft, whispering stillness.

Force leaves men hard and antagonistic. The still small voice is the expression of the "more excellent way." (1 Cor. 12:31.) The gentleness of God is winning souls by grace whom might and wrath have failed to move. O Lord, give us more of Your gentleness! Elijah came out of that cave not only with restored confidence, but with a changed nature. He was a better, nobler man. David expressed this transformation succinctly when he said of God: **Your gentleness has made me great** . . . . (Ps. 18:35 NKJ).

**The hearing ear and the seeing eye,
the Lord has made both of them.**

Proverbs 20:12 NKJ

This verse is only one of more than 17 I have counted in the Bible in which seeing and hearing are combined. It stresses that the Gospel is only complete when it is seen as well as heard. John says of Jesus that **. . . many believed in his name, when they** *saw* **the miracles which he did** (John 2:23).

For too long the Church in America has been on a "head-trip." We have placed emphasis on hearing about the faith — rather than on seeing faith in action today!

Too often Christians file out of church on Sunday morning, shake the pastor's hand and congratulate him on his good sermon, and then go their ways virtually unchanged. They may have accumulated and stored away more facts about the Gospel, but they have not really experienced the power of the Gospel. Week after week, this routine is repeated with no evidence of any real change in the lives of those who hear.

In the book of Acts, we read that the Holy Ghost fell on everyone who heard the Word. (Acts 10:44.) We also read that when the disciples preached the Word, the Lord worked with them to confirm that Word with miraculous signs. (Mark 16:20.) Paul said that his speaking was accompanied by powerful spiritual demonstration. (1 Cor. 2:4.)

I believe that before the coming of the Lord, the Church will once again preach the Gospel (for hearing) with the Holy Ghost sent down from heaven (for seeing). (1 Pet. 1:12.) Lord, hasten the day when we can see the Gospel with our eyes as well as hear it with our ears!

**. . . to those who are called, both Jews and Greeks,
Christ the power of God and the wisdom of God.**

1 Corinthians 1:24 NKJ

Power is something we can see with our eyes; wisdom is something we can hear with our ears. Jesus has both power and wisdom. He displayed His power in the miracles He performed; He demonstrated His wisdom in the words He spoke.

The Jewish people were impressed by miracles, signs and wonders, so they sought these as proof of divine origin. The Greeks were fascinated with knowledge, wisdom and understanding, so they sought these as evidence of deity. The pursuit of the Jew was emotional, that of the Greek was intellectual.

Jesus was able to satisfy the need of both Jew and Greek. He is still able. Whatever a person's background, culture, language, race, sex, or creed, Jesus can meet him right where he lives. Our Lord adapts Himself to each individual, regardless of that person's particular situation. Jesus is the power of God for those who need might as a point of contact. Jesus is the wisdom of God for those who need reason as a point of contact.

We want to win people powerfully and to win them wisely. Sensitivity to the person and his unique personality and make-up is so vital. The Holy Spirit can help us make the right adjustment to win each individual. Jesus was so full of His Father's *love* that people were impressed with His *wisdom* and *power.* (Matt. 13:54; Mark 6:2.) As His disciples, we are indwelt by the Source of all three of these qualities of love, wisdom and power: the Holy Spirit. (John 14:12; 1 Tim. 1:7.)

**". . . All the days of my hard service
I will wait, till my change comes."**

Job 14:14 NKJ

This verse contains the noun form of one of my favorite Hebrew verbs: *chalaph (khaw-laf')*. Here, Job is saying that despite his miserable condition, he is looking for a *change* of circumstance. E.W. Bullinger translates this phrase: ". . . I will wait until the time of my reviving comes." *The New International Version* renders it: ". . . I will wait for my renewal to come."

Unfortunately, Bible scholars have often assumed that Job was speaking of his dying. They read about death in the context and mistakenly conclude that Job's words deal with that subject. **Hard service** (or as the *King James Version* has it, "appointed time") is a military expression relating to engagement in warfare. All the time Job was waging the good fight of faith, he was not waiting for death but for a divine visitation. He was expecting a revival, a renewal, a change for the better. That change came when the Lord intervened to turn Job's captivity and reward his faithfulness with a double portion of all that he had lost in the hassle.

This can be our happy conclusion also. We too are engaged in the fight of faith. Our warfare against the powers of darkness goes on and on. We too look for a change, a renewal, a revival, a breakthrough. The Lord will intervene for us just as He did for Job.

Job expected changes in his circumstances. They came to him in double measure. We can expect the same. Get ready for dramatic changes in the whole Church world; they're coming. As the old song puts it: "There'll be some changes made today; there'll be some changes made!"

**But those who wait on the Lord
shall renew their strength . . . .**

Isaiah 40:31 NKJ

As noted in yesterday's lesson, one of my favorite Hebrew words is *chalaph (khaw-laf')*. It is a word that is used in various illustrative ways to indicate personality alteration, second growth, revival, renewal, and a change for the better.

When Mohammed died, his replacement was called a *caliph*, a derivative of this word *chalaph*. There is even conjecture by some scholars that California obtained its name from this Hebrew word. In the Middle Ages a novel was written about a mythical queen named California who took a desert wasteland and turned it into a beautiful garden. The *Calif* portion of her name was supposedly traced by some to *chalaph*.

In the original Hebrew version of this verse, the word translated **renew** is *chalaph*. In this case, it is defined as "exchange." We who wait on the Lord shall *exchange* our strength. Ours for His. What a beautiful picture!

In our time of trial, we can say: "Lord I am waiting for You, and while I am waiting something is happening. An exchange is taking place. My strength is being replaced by Your strength. My limited finances are giving way to Your riches in glory. My finite wisdom is being superseded by Your wisdom from above."

You can change every area of your life right now. Quote Isaiah 40:31 and tell the Lord that you want *chalaph*, a renewal, an exchange. If you want victory in your life, trade your resources for God's!

"And even now the ax is laid to
the root of the trees . . . ."
Matthew 3:10 NKJ

Part One

Here is a verse for dealing with genetic tendencies in a family tree. It assures us that there is an "ax" which can cut the "root" of cancer, alcoholism, stroke, heart attack, emotional disorder or any other inherited negative family trait. That ax, or cutting edge, is the Word of God which is **. . . living and powerful, and sharper than any two-edged sword, piercing even to the division of soul and spirit, and of joints and marrow . . . .** (Heb. 4:12 *NKJ*).

According to Scripture, God's blessings are passed down through a family for a thousand generations. (Ps. 105:8.) Defective tendencies will only reach to the third and fourth generations. (Ex. 20:5.) In view of that ratio, we ought to inherit a lot more "good stuff" than "bad stuff." However, it must be admitted that there are some negative family tendencies to be dealt with.

Some families have a history of cancer, some heart problems, some strokes, some insanity. Others have a marked tendency toward chemical addiction, lust, jealousy, worry, or bad temper. If there is any negative trait in your family tree, this verse is for you. Verbally state it as a confession of faith:

"Lord, Your Word is the cutting instrument. I lay the ax to the root of _____ in my family tree (fill in the word that characterizes your family tendency). *I claim freedom from the problems in my family which have been passed from one generation to the next. Thank You, Father, for this deliverance. Amen!"*

> **"For there is hope for a tree, if it is
> cut down, that it will sprout again, and
> that its tender shoots will not cease."**
>
> **Job 14:7** NKJ

Part Two

This is a continuation of yesterday's word: "Now the ax is laid to the root of the tree." Through the eyes of faith Job sees that the purpose of God's pruning is the removal of bad roots, not the chopping down of healthy trees. If the Lord went around cutting down every life that had a defect in it, there would not be many left standing — and I'm not at all sure that I would be one of them! Neither was the psalmist, evidently, for he asked this question of His Maker: **If You, Lord, should mark iniquities, O Lord, who could stand?** (Ps. 130:3 *NKJ*).

Here Job is talking about replacement. He is saying that, in the process of pruning, even if a tree were completely chopped down, there would still be hope of regrowth. That tree can **sprout again.** In the original Hebrew this expression is one word, *chalaph (khaw-laf')*, the word used for revival or renewal. Even though the ax is laid to the root of the tree, the tree itself can still revive. It can be renewed. It can come back again.

It should encourage us to know that the Lord can cut out of us every inherited genetic disturbance without destroying our lives. No matter how ingrained the cancer — the negative family trait or tendency — that root can be severed without destroying the life of the family tree. Though severely pruned, it will come back.

Tomorrow we will look at how the revived tree will be different and even better than the one it replaces.

He shall be like a tree planted
by the rivers of water . . . .
Psalm 1:3 NKJ

Part Three

The word **planted** in this verse is the Hebrew word *shatal (shaw-thal')*. In his concordance, Dr. James Strong uses a succinct and terse expression to define this root word: "to *transplant*." Thus this verse is a description of our new status as Christians. As subjects of the kingdom of God, you and I are "transplanted" trees.

Looking back over the past three days' lessons, we read: 1) "Now is the ax laid to the root of the trees." This verse had to do with severing genetic weaknesses from our lives; 2) "If the tree is cut down, there is hope that it will sprout again." We are promised a reviving and a renewal after our family tree is pruned; 3) "He shall be like a tree planted by the rivers of water." After our pruning, we the righteous will be like transplanted trees drawing directly from the rivers of divine life.

In these verses, the Lord is telling us that as new creatures in Christ, our renewed family tree will be better than ever. It will have plenty of moisture. It will be fruitful, and its foliage will not wither away.

All of us can go through this threefold process. Let's allow the Lord to 1) cut away anything in us that is detrimental to our Christian witness, 2) renew and revive our lives, and 3) manifest the fruit of the life of Christ in us as we draw from the water of life.

Our new transplanted life will result in abundant health, happiness, and harvest.

". . . from this day forward, I will bless you."
Haggai 2:19 NKJ

Have you ever seen the commercial slogan which asks the penetrating question, "Eventually, why not now?" Properly understood and applied, the message of that slogan can change our lives. There is a day of deliverance for every one of us, a day when God rends the heavens and intervenes on our behalf. According to this verse, for you and me that day is *today*!

Bringing our faith from futuristic hope and desire to present-tense "today-is-the-day!" expectation is not something that you and I can do in and of ourselves. "Only believe" is only possible when we have some solid basis for belief. All our optimism, enthusiasm, cliches, "buzz words," success slogans, positive mental attitudes, and even "confession of the Word" can be helpful. But the truth is that ultimately the only way you and I can believe strongly enough to transform future hope into present assurance is by *receiving a personal word directly from the Lord to us*. This verse is that word.

"From this day forward, I will bless you!" This verse not only promises us immediate deliverance today, it also enhances hope for tomorrow. "From this day forward" indicates that this is not a "one-time" blessing; this is a whole new way of life!

"Not only am I setting you free from all poverty, fear, sickness, trouble, and weakness," the Lord says to us, "but for the rest of your life I will continually bless you with good things." You and I have a lot to look forward to! Believe it and see!

**You shall increase my greatness,
and comfort me on every side.**

Psalm 71:21 NKJ

In the original Hebrew version, the word translated **comfort** is *nacham (naw-kham')*. It describes God's response to our trying circumstances.

One definition of *nacham* is "to sigh." The prophet Isaiah says of God and His people: **In all their affliction, he was afflicted . . . .** (Is. 63:9). The writer of Hebrews tells us that we have a High Priest Who is touched with the feelings of our infirmities. (Heb. 4:15.) So when circumstances cause us to sigh, the Lord sighs with us. But, He does infinitely more than that.

Another definition of *nacham* is "to breathe strongly" or "to draw breath forcibly." We do this in times of strong physical or emotional stress. We breathe hard when excited, when forced to move rapidly, or when the pace of our lives is drastically speeded up. When the Lord says through the psalmist that He will comfort us, He is saying that He will be right by our side. Our eagerness, excitement and enthusiasm become His eagerness, excitement, enthusiasm. In stressing that the spirit (Spirit) is *willing*, the Bible uses a word that describes ardent eagerness. Our God is just as eager for our victory as we are.

Another definition of *nacham* is "to pity," implying feeling such sorrow for a person as to step in and avenge him against his adversary. Gesenius, the grammarian, says of *nacham*: "It includes the notion of God putting forth help and taking vengeance."

Our God does much more than console us in our battles; He takes our side with us against our enemy!

. . . hope does not disappoint . . . .
Romans 5:5 NKJ

You have always known that God was going to answer your prayers. When you were unmarried, you knew that one day the Lord would bless you with a spouse and children. When your family members were still unsaved, you knew that someday they would all come to know the Lord. When your church was in need of revival, you knew that if you prayed with faith and patience, sooner or later that revival would break forth. You even knew that you would eventually get that much needed and deserved promotion and raise at work. You waited patiently to see these things (and other prayer requests) come to pass, because you had *hope* as an anchor for your soul. (Heb. 6:19.)

Hope is a good ingredient to have in our Christian character because it motivates us to keep going. When my wife and I accidentally drove our car off a hill and landed at the bottom of a ravine, it was the walk back up the side of that hill that told me how strong hope really is. I kept telling my wife while we were climbing, "Cars are only metal, glass, and rubber. We can always get another car, or even do without one if we have to. But there is one thing we have that no one can take away from us, and that is our hope and desire to go into all the world and preach the Gospel to every creature."

Hope keeps spiritual desire alive. It motivates us every day to get up and give life another try. It keeps us going when circumstances are screaming at us: "Give up! You'll never make it, why try any longer?"

Hope does not disappoint because it brings us to the point of our deliverance. The psalmist exhorts: **Be of good courage, and He shall strengthen your heart, all you who hope in the Lord** (Ps. 31:24 *NKJ*). Never give up!

**"Return to the stronghold, you prisoners of hope.
Even today I declare that I will restore double to you."**
Zechariah 9:12 NKJ

Prisoners of hope is an expression used to descibe those
who have waited a long, long time for a specific prayer to
be answered.

Actually, this expression is a bit misleading. In reality,
it is hope which is the prisoner. We lock it up in our hearts
and refuse to allow it to escape. The word **prisoners** in this
verse is a translation of a Hebrew word whose verb form
means "to tie down, to hold down, to bind in order to keep
in one place." Applied to a person or thing, our modern-
day equivalent might be "to put on hold." Hope is a very
good thing for us to "put on hold" in our hearts.

**Hope deferred makes the heart sick, but when the
desire comes, it is a tree of life** (Prov. 13:12 *NKJ*). What wise
Solomon meant here was that sometimes hope is not easy
to hold because it seems to cause us misery — until it is
fulfilled!

An airline attendant recognized me on a flight and told
me that eight years earlier in church I had given her a Scrip-
tural promise from the Lord that her husband would be
saved. She had locked that verse up in her heart and kept
it. Her husband's actions and lifestyle did not encourage her,
so she was tempted to give up. But she kept holding on to
the promise as a prisoner of hope. Later her husband was
not only saved, he began family devotions in the home, and
enrolled in a local Bible-study group. Her hope resulted in
a double "restoration": Salvation of her mate and a future
as the wife of a minister of the Gospel!

July 4

By pride comes only contention . . . .
Proverbs 13:10 NKJ

Much of earth's strife, conflict, turmoil, and war can be traced back to pride. It was a heart lifted up with pride that provoked the first war in all recorded history when Lucifer and his followers tried to overthrow the throne of the Most High. (Rev. 12:7; Ezek. 28:17.)

Pride always exalts self above true relationship to God. Contention results when pride drives a person furiously to "make it," even if it means crawling over others and clawing his way to the top.

Pride is behind virtually all misunderstandings, disagreements, differences, church squabbles, matrimonial friction, and family turmoil. The answer to pride is a healthy spirit of humility.

The word *humility* is always associated with lowliness. **. . . with the lowly is wisdom,** wrote the author of Proverbs 11:2. . . . **Mind not high things, but condescend to men of low estate . . . .,** counsels the great Apostle Paul in Romans 12:16. **Let the brother of low degree rejoice in that he is exalted,** says James in chapter one, verse nine, of the epistle by his name.

You and I can avoid the "hassle" of strife and conflict by heeding the words of wise Solomon: **Better it is to be of an humble spirit with the lowly, than to divide the spoil with the proud** (Prov. 16:19).

A truly humble person cannot be humiliated. How can you put down someone who is already low and sitting at the feet of Jesus?

**The more you are enriched the more scope
will there be for generous giving . . . .**
2 Corinthians 9:11 Phillips

Two things go with the Christian territory: gratitude and generosity.

Let's consider ourselves before our conversion. You and I were not born naturally grateful or generous. It was not our inherent nature either to esteem or praise others more than ourselves or to really enjoy giving away to others anything of real value to us. We weren't totally selfish, but then again we weren't totally unselfish either. We were just *self-centered.*

But then we were converted. To convert means "to turn around and go in the opposite direction." Now that we are heading in the opposite way, we have a new nature. Now that we are *Christ-centered,* we find it easy to give praise to God for His goodness and mercy to us and to praise other people for their efforts on our behalf. Likewise, we find it easy to give away material things. That giving starts a cycle of receiving which enables us to give even more. While we don't "give to get" (for ourselves), we do *give to get more to give.*

This verse assures us that the more we are enriched, the more scope we will have for generosity. Prosperity makes sense when it is motivated, not by selfishness, but by a sincere desire to bless others. The basic rule is: "Give, and it shall be given to you in return — and in abundance — so you will have more to give next time."

I believe that in the future we will see surface a large group of dedicated and committed believers who have a pronounced ministry of giving. I am convinced that Christians will become conspicuous by their generosity. Overflowing — *out*flowing — prosperity is on its way!

. . . **feed me with the food You prescribe for me.**
Proverbs 30:8 NKJ

This is the Old Testament equivalent of "Give us this
day our daily bread." With this verse from Proverbs, I was
able to lose twenty pounds.

As a result of spending a month in a very expensive
facility (paid for by an appreciative church group) and dining
on the tempting gourmet dishes provided me there, I found
myself overweight. More than that, I discovered that indulg-
ing my appetite had let it get totally out of control. I knew
I had to do something. Then I recalled this verse from a
previous weight-loss experience.

The *King James Version* reads: . . . **feed me food conve-**
nient for me. In this version the writer asks God for the food
which He prescribes. The Hebrew word translated **prescribe**
here is *choq (khoke)*. It is defined as "an appointment
combining time, labor, and usage." Elsewhere it is translated
"daily portion" or "daily bread."

The amount and type of food you and I need for the
average day depends upon the schedule and demands of
that particular day. I found that I could determine that
amount by a sensitivity to the promptings of the Holy Spirit.
Listening to the still small voice within enabled me to
recognize my daily need. Relying on the power of the Holy
Spirit strengthened me to consume only what was necessary
to fulfill that need. No more, no less. Such commitment
requires self-discipline, but the reward is well worth the
effort. When all the "fad diets" have failed, try the Lord's
prescribed plan: our daily bread.

The blessing of the Lord makes one rich, and He adds no sorrow with it.

Proverbs 10:22 NKJ

Here is an encouraging word from the Lord. It is an assurance that the good and beneficial blessings our Father bestows upon us will enrich our lives. In addition, He promises us help in avoiding the sorrow that often goes with earthly increase and promotion.

In the original version, the Hebrew word translated **sorrow** is *'etseb (eh'-tseb)* and is defined as "physical toil, emotional pain and anguish, mental fatigue and discomfort." On the human level, advancement often leads to problems. In our world, the higher a person climbs up the ladder of success, the more risks he encounters. Many times, the inner price of outer success is a heavy one indeed.

In this verse, wise Solomon assures us that it is not so in the kingdom of God. Our loving Father blesses and enriches His children while at the same time deflecting any grief that might tend to accompany and spoil the joy of His benedictions.

It is as though the Lord is saying to us: "My blessings are not sweet and sour. I am not going to make you both happy and miserable. I do not open My hand to pour out blessing and sorrow at the same time."

One scholar has written concerning this verse: "Whatever we receive in the way of providential benefits has God's blessing in it and will do us good. Cares, troubles, and difficulties come with all property not acquired in this way. God's blessing gives simple enjoyment and levies no taxes upon the comfort we receive."

**Do not lie in wait, O wicked man,
against the dwelling of the righteous;
do not plunder his resting place.**
Proverbs 24:15 NKJ

This verse speaks directly to those who break into people's homes to steal and vandalize. It warns them against trespassing on the premises of the righteous.

Law enforcement agencies claim that one out of seven homes in the United States will be broken into this year. The media tells us that in New York City, the most common "status symbol" is an elaborate security system consisting of seven chains, locks, bars, dead-bolts, barriers, and door restrainers. One writer there reported pathetically that it takes him nearly fifteen minutes to disengage his anti-burglar system so he can open his front door.

As believers, this verse is given to assure us that there is something better than all that protective paraphernalia. Our trust in God Almighty provides us a peace and assurance unknown to those outside the Lord.

The Bible tells us that the angel of the Lord encamps about those who reverence and respect Him. (Ps. 34:7.) For us Christians, there is a better way. Our protection is not physical, but spiritual. We could call it "the celestial security system"! Try it, it works!

**. . . let us continually offer the sacrifice
of praise to God, that is, the fruit of our
lips, giving thanks to His name.**

Hebrews 13:15 NKJ

A sacrifice is something of value which is freely given up by one person in order to please, enhance, or benefit another. Jesus' death on the cross is an example of the supreme sacrifice. He freely offered up His life for us human beings in order to accomplish for us what we could never do for ourselves, pay the full price of our redemption from our sins.

The sacrifice of praise is something we offer up to our Lord. A sacrifice requires self-denial. Just as Jesus voluntarily gave up His life for our sakes, though He despised the cross, so we give Him the praise and thanksgiving due Him, though we may not always feel like doing so.

If ours is to be a true sacrifice, we cannot wait for favorable circumstances before we offer it. We are to offer up praise and thanks continually. Such praise is not always a sincere expression of the heart. Sometimes the fruit of our lips can be the most shallow effort imaginable. Phonetically, all the lips can do is enunciate sounds. Those sounds alone do not necessarily constitute true praise. It is when the lips overflow with that which is welling up in our innermost being that we produce the real fruit of praise.

However, even if our praise does seem superficial and shallow, it is still highly acceptable as a sacrifice to the Lord. God does not require us to feel, only to acknowledge: **Let every thing that hath breath praise the Lord** (Ps. 150:6).

Instead of the thorn shall come up the fir tree, and instead of the brier shall come up the myrtle tree . . . .
Isaiah 55:13

This is one of those before and after verses. It describes you and me before and after our conversion. It stresses the difference between life without the Spirit and life filled with the Spirit.

The thorn describes the unregenerate man. A thorn tree grows like a weed without cultivation; it has no utility, no beauty or redeeming features. A thorn punctures and irritates. Thorns go with the wasteland, this wilderness we call the world.

The fir tree, on the other hand, is a picture of the regenerated man. It is an evergreen. Green is the color of eternal life. Thus the evergreen is symbolic of salvation. The fir does not fade; all year long its needles and branches point right up toward heaven. Instead of being thorn trees in the wilderness, you and I are living fir trees, perpetually straight and green and lively.

The brier represents the dead and barren life without the Spirit. The brier is a good picture of the self-life: uncrucified, unruly, undisciplined.

The myrtle represents life with the Spirit. The myrtle is known for its aroma. The fragrance of righteousness, love, and eternal life replaces the stench of worldliness, selfishness, and death.

All this life, beauty, and fragrance is worth receiving!

. . . Judah shall again take root
downward, and bear fruit upward.

Isaiah 37:31 NKJ

A tree grows in three directions: downward, upward, and outward. This verse promises growth and expansion in two of the three directions, both down and up at the same time. The message is that our growth as Christians is recognizable by ourselves, by the Lord's angelic host, and by others as well.

Taking root downward is progess known only to us. The root system is below the surface and not visible to anyone. In the course of a year, there is growth, but it is undetected. You and I are not the same people we were a year ago. Perhaps others cannot see the deepening process at work, but we know it is there.

Bearing fruit upward has visible results. Fruit bearing is an activity that is open and apparent to any observer. Fruit is the end result of a year's special effort. It is for all to see and enjoy.

Bearing fruit is also another word for productivity. When Jesus said that we would be able to judge a tree by its fruit, He was telling us to be observant of our own lives, as well as others', because we show what we are by what we produce.

The ring on the inside of a tree may be minuscule and totally hidden from human view. But year in and year out, it records a message: this tree is growing and producing fruit. Visible and invisible growth is taking place.

You and I should be encouraged! The Lord has promised us continuous and on-going growth!

"I have been crucified with Christ; it is no longer I who live, but Christ lives in me . . . ."
Galatians 2:20 NKJ

The usual Greek word translated *crucified* is *stauroo (stow-ro-o)* meaning "to impale on a cross." Here in this verse, Paul uses the Greek word *sustauroo (soos-tow-ro-o)*, "to impale in company with," referring to a co-crucifixion. This is the word used for the two thieves who were crucified along with Jesus.

Paul stresses that he was also impaled on the cross with Jesus. When Christ died, Paul died with Him. But like Christ, Paul did not stay dead. If Paul was crucified and buried with Christ, he was also raised to new life with Christ. The remainder of this verse declares: **". . . and the life which I now live in the flesh I live by faith . . . ."** The apostle understood that his old life "*of* the flesh" was gone and the life he now lived "*in* the flesh" was a spiritual one.

Paul's new life was totally different from that which he had lived before the crucifixion of his "old man." The same is true of you and me. We too were crucified, dead and buried with our Lord. We too were raised to new life in Christ. Christ is seated in the heavenlies, and Paul tells us that we are seated there with Him. (Eph. 1:3.) If that is so, if we are new spiritual beings, what kind of life should we now live?

Men have spent centuries focusing on our need to be crucified with Christ, to nail our "old man" to the cross. But the co-crucifixion is not the end, the ultimate achievement, or the final goal. It is simply God's ordained method for getting us into *resurrection life*. As Paul said of himself, you and I can say of ourselves: we are *dead to sin, but alive in Christ!*

**They willingly received Him into the boat,
and immediately the boat was at the
land where they were going.**

John 6:21 NKJ

Two things happened at once when Jesus stepped on board the disciples' boat: 1) the storm ceased, and 2) the boat landed at the shore to which the disciples were headed.

There is a very important message for all of us in this story. The Lake of Galilee is six to eight miles across. Having been born and reared in this area, no doubt the disciples were in familiar territory. They had set out from the eastern side of the lake at about 6 p.m., intending to cross over to the western shore.

As they made the crossing, suddenly a storm came up and their passage became extremely difficult. They rowed until 3 a.m. and had only been able to cover three or four miles. That is when they saw Jesus coming toward them, walking on the water.

After six to nine hours of exhaustive toil, they were only halfway across the lake. In the midst of the storm, in the middle of the lake, Jesus stepped on board their ship. When His feet touched the deck, immediately the storm was calmed and the boat landed on the other shore.

This may be a picture of your life right now. It may seem that you have been rowing forever, and yet are still far from shore. In the midst of your storms and toil, invite Jesus to come aboard. He will still the storm and get you to your destination far quicker than you could ever imagine!

**Now in the morning, as He returned to the city,
He was hungry. And seeing a fig tree by the road,
He came to it and found nothing on it but leaves,
and said to it, "Let no fruit grow on you ever
again." And immediately the fig tree withered away.**

Matthew 21:18,19 NKJ

During their travels, Jesus and the disciples, looking for
nourishment, came to a fig tree . To their disappointment,
the tree had leaves but no fruit. Jesus spoke to the tree, and
it died and withered away.

Some critical writers feel that Jesus' cursing the tree is
out of character. Their rationale is: "Jesus went about doing
good. Why does He now reverse field and go in an opposite
direction? Why cursing instead of blessing?"

Utility is the word. In the economy of God, all living
organisms function to produce and reproduce. This tree was
occupying space in an already crowded world. Its roots were
taking valuable nutrients out of the soil. Its branches were
soaking up sunshine. Its leaves were drinking in rain. The
tree was taking in but not giving out. It was serving no
purpose, yet was draining resources. So the Creator removed
it by speaking to it harshly.

Fear, poverty, insecurity, bodily ailments — anything
negative or debilitating, anything that takes up time, space,
or energy without producing positive results — can be
removed from our lives. Our Lord has promised to prune
us, to cut away everything from us which has no utility,
purpose, or benefit. (John 15:2.) With this assurance, we can
concentrate more fully on the areas of our life that are fruit-
ful and productive.

**. . the God of peace will crush Satan
under your feet shortly . . . .**

Romans 16:20 NKJ

The two key words here are: **crush** and **shortly.** One tells us how thoroughly powerless our enemy has been made since his defeat at Calvary; **crush** indicates total destruction. The other tells us how soon we can expect to see this destruction; **shortly** indicates that we do not have long to wait.

In the original Greek text, the word translated **crush** (**bruise** in the *King James Version*) is *suntribo (soon-treé-bo)*, which is a verb meaning "to crush completely; to shatter; to break in pieces; to pulverize, disintegrate, torpedo, annihilate." This word presents an image of all the works of the enemy being thoroughly taken apart. What a promise of victory for the Christian.

In the original, **shortly** is an expression made up of two Greek words: *en (en)* and *tachos (tahk-os)*. It is defined as "in haste, as soon as possible, without delay, suddenly, swiftly, with all speed." This too is encouraging to the believer.

Do you have problems? Quote this verse as a confession of faith: "The God of peace is going to shatter the enemy under my feet without delay. In Luke 10:19 my Lord has promised that I will tread on Satan and his demons. My feet are shod with the gospel of peace. I am ready for the imminent victory — right now — in Jesus' name!"

There is one who speaks like the piercings of a sword, but the tongue of the wise promotes health.

Proverbs 12:18 NKJ

I meet people everywhere I go who were raised in a climate of sarcasm. All they ever heard were cutting, belittling, abrasive words. On the outside, such people may appear unharmed, but inside they are still bruised, cut, and bleeding. Unless they find healing, that invisible hurt will usually make its presence known and felt in one negative way or another.

We Christians must be on our guard against sarcasm. Because of its powerful negative effect, this word is worth examining. According to *Webster's New Twentieth Century Dictionary,* it comes from the Greek word *sarcasmos,* which is a derivative of *sarkazein,* meaning "to tear flesh like dogs."

This verse tells us that sarcastic speech pierces like a sword. Sarcastic people can cut you to pieces with their tongues. Their words tear to shreds, wounding the "flesh" — and especially the *spirit* — of their victims.

But the verse ends on a positive note: . . . **the tongue of the wise promotes health.** Our words can cut or they can mend. They can wound, or they can heal. They can tear down or build up. We have a choice: we can pierce with sarcasm, or we can heal with words of wisdom.

Luke tells us that the people were astonished at the gracious words that came out of Jesus' mouth. (Luke 4:22.) What a role model He was! Following our Lord's example, we can always speak healing words. Let's do it!

**". . . the mountains and hills will burst
into song before you, and all the trees of
the field will clap their hands."**

Isaiah 55:12b NIV

We know that the earth we live in can respond to the kind of treatment we give it. In Genesis 4:10, the blood of Abel (recently murdered) cried out from the ground on which it had been spilled. The Red Sea parted to allow the children of Israel to march through to safety. When Solomon was dedicated and anointed king, the very ground on which he was standing shook by reason of the occasion.

In Revelation 12:16 we read in symbolic language that during future times, the earth will help the woman and will swallow the flood of persecution that comes forth from the mouth of the dragon. Scripture also tells us that the earth is affected by the sin and depravity of humanity. Paul writes that the whole creation groans and travails under the burden of mankind's fallen state. (Rom. 8:21,22.)

In this verse, the prophet says that mountains and hills will "break forth into singing" and the trees of the field will "clap their hands." The earth responds favorably to the proclamation of the Good News. Mountains and hills are symbolic of permanence and strength. All of life is not quicksand, barren wilderness, or dry desert; some of it is tree covered. Trees represent growth, beauty, and fruitfulness. Even the mountains and trees will rejoice at our coming to announce the Good News of Jesus Christ.

Can you imagine what kind of desolate wasteland this world would be without the Gospel or its messengers?

**"For you shall go out with joy,
and be led out with peace . . . ."**
Isaiah 55:12a NKJ

The first time this verse ever came to me was in a moment of great need. I had just graduated from a Bible school with an evangelistic call on my life. Only one door opened to my wife and me. An invitation came to hold several meetings, but there were problems.

We had a small, light, ten-year-old car, which was totally incapable of making the long trip from California to the Colorado mountain town to which we had been invited. In order to accept the invitation, we knew that we would have to sell our old car and purchase a newer one and a travel trailer. Realizing we needed divine help, we parked the car by an open field in the San Fernando Valley and prayed to the Lord for guidance, direction, and assistance. A peaceful calm filled the car and this verse came to us: **". . . you shall go out with joy, and be led out with peace . . . ."** Immediately our outlook changed from reticent uncertainty to confident assurance.

In the next 90 days the Lord restructured our transportation system by supplying us with a newer, heavier car and a travel trailer. He also sent us the cash we needed for travel expenses. We made the trip and arrived safe and sound and ready for revival. The joy and peace that accompanied us was very real.

This verse knows no geographical limitation, time restriction, financial hindrance, physical confinement, or legal blockage. It applies equally to everyone who is working for the Lord and doing His will. It is a word just for *you*!

**For you shall not go out with haste,
nor go by flight . . . .**

Isaiah 52:12a NKJ

The two key words here are **haste** and **flight.** They need to be defined because both words speak volumes to us in understanding the Lord's leadings and dealings with us.

Haste is a word which implies compulsive action. It suggests being on the run due to guilt, fear, or anxiety. A verse that describes the impulsiveness and impetuousness inherent in those who act hastily is Proverbs 28:1: **The wicked flee when no one pursues . . . .** (*NKJ*).

You and I, being led by the Spirit of the Lord, never have to make decisions or take actions motivated by guilt or fear. The way our loving Father leads us is by the reassuring words from His book and by the calm and encouraging workings of His Holy Spirit.

Flight is easily understood by adding a "y" and changing it into *flighty.* Webster defines this word as "given to flights or sallies of fancy, caprice, etc; volatile; frivolous; slightly delirious; light-headed; mildly crazy." A flighty person is unstable, always trying to escape reality by trips into the world of the imagination or wishful thinking.

Led by the Lord, you and I will never have to go anywhere motivated by guilt, fear, or nervous unrest. Isaiah tells us that we will go out with joy and be led forth with peace. (Is. 55:12.) What a difference there is between going with fear, anxiety, or capriciousness and going forth with joy and peace. Our choice is the latter! I know it's your choice too!

> . . . for the Lord will go before you, and
> the God of Israel will be your rear guard.

Isaiah 52:12b NKJ

Every group of travelers has two kinds of people: fast movers and slow movers. Fast movers are aggressive, ambitious, alert, and highly motivated to move out and get on with the journey. Slow movers tend to dawdle, waver, hesitate, to be unsure, reticent, or indecisive. It is very difficult to lead any group of people when part of them are forever rushing ahead while another part is always lagging behind.

This verse says that the Lord is out in front of the self-motivated marchers, and He is also following up at the rear of the stragglers. David calls attention to the fact that the Lord both goes ahead and follows up when he says of Him, **You have hedged me behind and before . . . .** (Ps. 139:5).

It is a comfort to know that our God is present in both areas of our lives. He is "riding point" out in front of us leading the way, and He is our rear guard protecting us from being picked off by the enemy.

The *King James Version* uses an archaic word for rear guard. *Rereward,* a holdover from antiquity, is derived from a word meaning "to gather together." No matter where we are positioned in the army of the Lord — front line or rear echelon — we are safe. The Lord is in both areas watching over us!

The Lord has made bare His holy arm in the eyes of all the nations; and all the ends of the earth shall see the salvation of our God.

Isaiah 52:10 NKJ

This verse combines the past and the future. The Lord *has* bared His arm and the earth *shall* see His salvation.

The baring of the arm of the Lord took place at the crucifixion of Christ. The ends of the earth began to see the salvation of the Lord at the resurrection of Jesus and will continue to witness the ongoing of that salvation until it is complete. The baring of God's arm has been accomplished, but the vision of His salvation is not yet totally realized.

At the crucifixion of Jesus, the whole world was represented. People from over 70 nations were present in Jerusalem because of the Jewish passover feast. The ruling government of Rome set the stage. The Greek culture provided the language used by the principal players. The Hebrew religionists were present to act out their parts. The drama unfolded, as the arm of the Lord was made bare.

You and I enter into this, the greatest drama of human history, by volunteering to take the Good News of man's redemption to the very ends of the earth. That Good News has not thoroughly penetrated every corner of the globe, but it will. We all have a role to play in the thrilling fulfillment of this verse. Each of us must do our part to see to it that . . . **all the ends of the earth shall see the salvation of our God!**

**"Although your beginning may seem small,
He will make your later years very great."**
Job 8:7 MLB

This verse promises us a good, vigorous, productive, fruitful, and expanding future. It is an assurance that God can do great things with our lives no matter how insignificant our beginnings. History records the success of many famous people who began life in the most humble of settings. One of these is the Lord Jesus Christ.

There is something about life that challenges people to raise their level of desire and expectation. The story of our own Christian lives actually begins with us deep in sin. Then salvation lifts us up out of the muck and sets our feet on the firm rock of the Son of God. Sanctification replaces our filthy garments of pride and self-righteousness with the dazzling white robes of His righteousness. The Holy Spirit gives us the power to run the race of life that is set before us and to gain the victory in the good fight of faith. At the close of the battle, we are each given a wedding garment. The story ends with us — the Bride of Christ — being enthroned with Him next to the Father. (Rev. 3:21.)

Our beginning can be compared to a mustard seed — small and insignificant. Our ending is centered in the universal acclaim of Jesus as Lord of the whole creation.

Christians have so much to look forward to. Our best days are yet to come!

... **my cup runneth over.**

Psalm 23:5

In Psalm 66:12, David writes of His God: **. . . thou broughtest us out into a wealthy place.** The Hebrew word translated **wealthy** in that context is the same Hebrew word translated **runneth over** in this verse. The word is *revayah (rev-aw-yah')* which has to do with an abundance of moisture. This abundance is so overflowing it satisfies all thirst so that the person becomes saturated or satiated.

In Psalm 66:12, David notes that after having been submerged (inundated) by men, fire, and flood, the people of Israel had been brought by their God to a place of overflowing *(rev-aw-yah')* abundance and blessing. The psalmist exults in the Lord's tender loving shepherd's care for him and his people. His cup is saturated to overflowing *(revayah)*. He is experiencing more than a sufficiency of God's wonderful blessings in his life.

Do you think it is possible to live this way today? We hear people say, "I'm just hanging in there," or, "If I can just make it to payday," or, "I'm just getting by, just holding on!" Do such statements reveal the presence of an overflowing abundance in these people's lives?

Revayah indicates living in a realm of abundant blessing. It suggests having not only a cup of your own, but having that cup full to overflowing. The overflow always becomes a surplus to share with others.

Deliver us, Lord, from all the restrictions we put on Your bountifulness!

. . . Go in this thy might . . .: have not I sent thee?
Judges 6:14

God's commands are also His enablements. When He says to do something, He imparts the ability to do it. In this verse, He is telling Gideon to go, and to expect unusual things to happen as he does.

The Lord is not saying, "Go, just to be doing something. Keep busy and you'll stay out of trouble." Rather, He is ordering Gideon out on the cutting edge of the unusual. The unexpected and the extraordinary are embodied in this little word *go*.

"Go in this thy *might*." In the original Hebrew from which this text was translated, this word is quite unusual. *Kowach (ko-akh)* is defined as "capacity, means, substance, wealth, or ability." So what the Lord was telling Gideon was, "Go in your ability; I am well aware it is not sufficient for the task I am sending you to accomplish, but don't worry about that because I am going with you to see that it gets done!"

As Christians, our function in life is very similar to that of Gideon. We too have a special touch of God on our lives. We are not here to duplicate, imitate, or copy anyone else in this world. By doing God's will, following His leadings, obeying His voice, like Gideon of old we too are assured of having all the power and resources of heaven behind us. To go is to be guaranteed the glorious presence of the Lord with us. When God goes into operation, phenomenal things begin to happen!

"Take what you have and go where I send you, because as you go I will go with you!" (Matt. 28:20; Mark 16:20.)

**And when the Chief Shepherd appears, you will
receive the crown of glory that will never fade away.**

1 Peter 5:4 NIV

The title Chief Shepherd is a very interesting descrip-
tion of Jesus. *Archipoimen (ar-khee-poy'-mane)* compounds two
Greek words: *arche (ar-khay')*, meaning "commencement,
first, beginning, author, principle"; and *poimen (poy-mane')*,
meaning "pastor, shepherd."

Jesus is our Chief (Primary) Shepherd. All other church
leaders are under-shepherds who lead us to Christ, the Head
of the Church. Under-shepherds also lead us in behalf of
Christ as His appointed representatives. Thus, our pastors
lead us *to* Christ, and they also lead us *for* Christ.

Jesus is Chief Shepherd because He originated our faith.
He authored it and perfects it. (Heb. 12:2 *NIV.*)

Jesus is Chief Shepherd because He leads us to God,
to salvation and eternal life. (John 14:6; John 10:7-18.) By clear-
ing the road, He insures all of us that once we have begun
the journey of faith, we can be assured of reaching our final
destination safely.

Jesus is also Chief Shepherd because by His atoning
death and triumphant resurrection, He earned the right to
be Head of the Church. (Phil. 2:9-11; Eph. 5:23.)

Jesus is the power-center of the universe. He is also the
role model we can safely look to and follow. He chose twelve
champions who were willing to give up their lives to follow
a Super-Champion. He puts shepherds in each congrega-
tion to lead the flock to the Chief Shepherd so He can lead
us home!

**"Although your beginning may seem small,
He will make your later years very great."**

Job 8:7 MLB

We have already looked at this verse on another day. There is one word in it, however, that needs to be scrutinized. The *King James Version* reads: **. . . thy latter days** (the last years of your life) **should greatly increase.** In the original Hebrew text, the word translated **greatly** is *me'od (meh-ode')* and has a certain intensity about it. *Me'od* means "vehemence, speedily, with rapid acceleration."

Look at an airplane going down the runway. For a time it looks as though it is barely moving. Then it begins to pick up speed. The really exciting part of the takeoff is the moment of liftoff. The plane leaves the ground and rapidly begins its ascent into the sky. *Me'od* is the word that the ancient Hebrews would have used to describe the acceleration and liftoff of a modern-day jetliner.

For a long time now you have been in motion. For all your efforts, it doesn't seem that you have gone anywhere. Despite your lack of progress, you have kept trying. You haven't quit. You have kept on "giving it your best shot." Very soon now, a new acceleration and thrust is going to take over. Before you know it, you are going to be off and climbing, soaring to worlds unknown. All this is promised you in this verse.

Paraphrased, it comes out: "Your start may seem to you quite small and insignificant. But very soon now, and very suddenly, you will be propelled by the Lord into a larger and greater sphere of influence."

The literal Hebrew reads: "Your start was small, your future shall rapidly increase." Praise the Lord!

**You number my wanderings; put my tears
into Your bottle; are they not in Your book?**

Psalm 56:8 NKJ

God keeps very accurate records. Not only does He
record our thoughts, words, and deeds, He also keeps
account of our tears. This verse tells us that they are all
recorded, stored up, and filed away in heaven's treasury. Two
types of tears are especially dear to God:

TEARS OF INTERCESSION. Jesus wept over Jerusalem.
John Knox shed tears over his beloved Scotland. Evan
Roberts interceded for Wales with tears. Charles Finney shed
tears for the dreadful plight of Colonial America. All tears
shed in intercession are kept for a memorial.

TEARS OF JOY. Whenever a prodigal returns home, a
loved one is born again, a lost sheep is found, it is quite
natural for tears of joy to well up and flow out. These tears
are also kept for a memorial.

A man once came to our town who was billed as "the
man who can neither smile nor cry." A reward was offered
to anyone who could bring a smile to his face or tears to
his eyes. No one collected. It was sad in a way to see people
follow him around, trying in vain to make him respond.
There was no reward for their efforts but a lonely vacant look
in his eyes.

Tears are an indication of a tender heart. Hard-hearted
people cannot weep. It is a spiritual distinctive to be so
sensitive, so tender, that you can rejoice with those who
rejoice and weep with those who weep. (Rom. 12:15.)

All our tears are kept as a memorial for us. They are
not gone, we will meet them again. One day we will be
rewarded by them and for them. O blessed day!

**May my prayer be counted as incense
before Thee . . . .**

Psalm 141:2 NASB

Here is a verse that speaks to people who are unable to go to the Lord's house for worship due to unfavorable circumstances. The psalmist David was fleeing from King Saul and could not go to the synagogue or temple for regular worship. These words in Psalm 141 express his desire to be a worshipper even though deprived of entrance into the house of the Lord.

During World War II, our military base was put on a three- to four-month alert. From 6 a.m. to 6 p.m., seven days a week, we were busy preparing for the North African invasion. The first thing I missed was worship in the house of the Lord and the fellowship of the saints. Necessity brought a few brothers in the Lord together for prayer and fellowship. Since then I have had a real compassion for people who are unable to go to church.

In his commentary on the Bible, Adam Clarke comments on this verse: "The psalmist appears to have been at this time at a distance from the sanctuary, and therefore could not perform the Divine worship in the way prescribed by the law. What could he do? Why, as he could not worship God according to the letter of the law, he will worship God according to the spirit; then prayer is accepted in the place of incense; and the lifting up of his hands, in gratitude and self-dedication to God, is accepted in the place of the evening minchah or oblation."

The lesson is: If you cannot go to the sanctuary, you can still offer up the sacrifice of praise and the incense of prayer.

**". . . the owner of a house . . . brings out of
his storeroom new treasures as well as old."**
Matthew 13:52 NIV

Part One

This is a balance verse. It tells us that we do not have
to choose between old and new. We can have both. In a
world given to choosing up sides, it is good to know that
we can reap the benefits of both sides. The kingdom of God
is not an either/or proposition. It is both old and new.

Old is a good word because it means "time-honored,
time-tested, time-proven." In this setting, *old* doesn't denote
that which is obsolete, archaic, or worn out. Rather, it
suggests paths that are well trodden; truths that have stood
the test of time; ways, customs and traditions that are
familiar, meaningful, dependable.

A geyser is called "Old Faithful." A dog lover calls his
faithful pet "Old Shep." A proud nation symbolically calls
its flag "Old Glory."

The householder, representing the Christian, brings out
of his pantry old, basic, reliable staples for his menu. The
Lord does the same for us: the blood of Jesus, the name of
the Lord, the power of the Holy Spirit, the effectiveness of
prayer, the preciousness of worship, the warmth of
fellowship.

If fasting and prayer brought revival 150 years ago, they
will do the same today. If songs of praise produced the
presence of the Lord in the Welsh revival of 1904, they will
do that for us today. The message of this verse is: "Don't
discard the old in order to be ready for the new. God's
treasures are like new edifices laid on the old foundations!"

". . . the owner of a house . . . brings out of his storeroom new treasures as well as old."

Matthew 13:52 NIV

Part Two

Yesterday's article spoke of the value of the "old" treasures. In addition to time-honored and trustworthy truths, the Lord has some "new" truths for us. In the Old Testament, the word *new* has the connotation of something fresh, exhilarating, invigorating. One translation of it is "fresh and green." "Having life," "being supple and vibrant," and "having a growth potential" all describe this word *new.*

Changes do not come easy to the church world, yet it must change in order to keep up with the Holy Spirit. Changes do not come easy to individuals, yet the Lord wants us to be receptive to all the new things He offers:

NEW WINE: Predictable Christianity reduces our service to the Lord to sameness, tameness, and lameness. New wine gladdens the heart. It brings new life, spontaneity, and the release of God's creativity.

NEW ANOINTING: In Psalm 92:10 David writes: **. . . I shall be anointed with fresh** ("new") **oil.** The Lord has a new touch of His Spirit to place in our lives.

NEW HEART: God has promised to replace our calloused, stony heart with a new heart of flesh. (Ezek. 36:26.) You will always know when you have a new heart by the attitude change that comes to you.

We have been promised a new name, a new strength, new tongues, new direction, new blessings, a new heaven, and a new earth. Let's retain and esteem the old things of God, but let's also be open to all the new things the Lord has prepared for us.

". . . the owner of a house . . . brings out of his storeroom new treasures as well as old."

Matthew 13:52 NIV

Part Three

An old song was sung about "Poor Johnny One-Note." He had a great voice, but he could only produce one note. Every time he got up to sing, out came that one sound. It wasn't long before everyone became tired of continuously hearing Johnny's one musical repertoire.

In the church world, it is common for an evangelist, a pastor, or a teacher to become a "Johnny One-Note." It is so easy to find a favorite subject or a pet theme and to ride it to death.

Early in his Christian life, the new believer begins to discover that there is a whole new world of spiritual knowledge available to him. As he listens, reads, meditates, and studies, the Holy Spirit reveals to him many wonderful, exciting truths about God's nature and man's potential. The problem develops when the believer settles down and begins to major on one particular truth to the exclusion of all others.

Ours is a God of infinite variety. His wisdom is many-hued and multi-faceted. He wants you and me to be open to ever new manifestations of His glory and power. In 1707 A.D., in his expository notes on the New Testament, William Burkett, commenting on this verse, noted that a household steward must provide (food) for the household both with plenty and with variety. He brings out of the treasury in plenty ". . . *Things new and old*, for their Variety . . . . he must be prudent, in bringing things new, as well as old; . . . lest the Household by always feeding upon the same Dish, do nauseate it, instead of being nourished by it."

Let's balance our lives with new as well as old.

Are the consolations of God too small for you, and the word *spoken* gently with you?

Job 15:11 NKJ

God's gentle nature never changes. His patient attributes are immutable, His kindly ways past finding out. In the process of time, His gentle words sensitize us into recognizing His patient dealings with us.

We may be expecting a more harsh, severe response when we fail our Lord, but He is working on our development. His plan is to improve us by working out our carnality and working in His spirituality. **The word *spoken* gently** will tug at our heart strings and produce a Christ-like response in us.

To my great regret, I once used the name of the Lord in an outburst of profanity. I was 16 at the time and tried to impress a group of guys by using coarse language. Not only were the guys not impressed, the Lord spoke gently to me and said, "You have hurt Me." That gentle word broke me up so much that I vowed never again to use God's name in vain or profanely.

In other situations I have made snap judgments, or acted impulsively, impatiently, or impetuously. Instead of "raking me over the coals of His righteous indignation," the Lord would simply speak a gentle word of reproof. He would let me know that such behavior was offensive to Him. He would show me what I had done wrong. Then He would give me godly sorrow for my sins, lead me to a heart-felt confession of my wrongdoing, and restore me to fellowship by His reconciliation.

God's gentleness is a salve or precious ointment to be applied to our spiritual man when we are hurting because of mistakes we have made.

**"You did not choose Me, but I
chose you and appointed you . . . ."**

John 15:16 NKJ

This verse can be a great source of encouragement to each of us. God, at the beginning of creation, looked down the telescope of time and saw every person who would ever exist. For His own purposes, and for His honor, He selected those who would bring glory to His name. These He set aside for Himself, calling them vessels of honor.

As Christians, children of God, beloved of the Father, each of us has been individually chosen and appointed as . . . **a vessel for honor** (2 Tim. 2:21 NKJ).

In Deuteronomy 18:4,5, the Lord told the children of Israel why He had selected them as His people. It was not because of their size; the other nations around them were much larger in territory and number. Nor was His choice based on any goodness or excellence on their part; in their wilderness rebellions they constantly provoked Him to the point of totally destroying them. God did not choose Israel because of their good looks, wealth, achievement, or intelligence. He chose them because He had given His word of covenant to Abraham, Isaac, and Jacob. Why He chose Abraham (and us) on whom to bestow His promise of blessing is still a mystery to us.

For us to attempt to itemize all the reasons why the Lord might have chosen us would be to miss completely the message of this verse and all those which speak of our election. Such verses are recorded to give us "humble boldness." Boldness to know that we are included in the number of God's redeemed. Humility to know that it was not we who chose Him, but He who loved us, knew us, and chose us — from the foundation of the world. (Eph. 1:4.)

"If you abide in Me, and My words abide in you, you will ask what you desire, and it shall be done for you."

John 15:7 NKJ

Part One

This verse points out the benefits of abiding in the Lord and of His words abiding in us. This word **abide** suggests taking up residence in a place for the purpose of making it a permanent home. As believers, our true homeland is the kingdom of God, which is spiritual, not material. The kingdom is *within us.* (Luke 17:21.)

We abide in the Lord by believing, serving, obeying, submitting to and following after *Him* — the Person, the Sovereign, the King. The idea is that as children of the Living Lord, we have a new family, location, sphere of influence, and Source: "If you will settle down in *Me*, and all that I represent, and if you will allow *My words* to settle down in you, then you will be able to ask what you will in confident assurance that it will be granted."

The Lord's **words** which are to abide in us, in addition to written Scriptures, are His *rhema (rhay'-ma)*, His *utterance*, His spoken words to us personally and individually. Hearing these words spoken directly to us into our own ears by the Spirit of God is the basis for guidance and confident assurance in our praying. *The key to answered prayer is knowing what to ask for!* That knowledge comes from *hearing* the *rhema* (the Voice) of God personally, speaking the Word to us by His Spirit. (Rom. 10:17.)

This verse challenges us: 1) to settle down in the kingdom, and 2) to allow God's words *to* us to settle down and take root *in* us. Then, and only then, are we ready to start making requests of the reigning Monarch.

"If you abide in Me, and My words abide in you, you will ask what you desire, and it shall be done for you."

John 15:7 NKJ

Part Two

The word **ask** in this verse is an interesting one. In the original Greek, it is *aiteo (ahee-teh'-o)* meaning to "ask, beg, call for, crave, desire, require." Because of its usage in Matthew 5:42, some Bible scholars have interpreted it to mean to "demand." In that verse, the Lord Jesus was emphasizing that a rude, insensitive, boorish person can ask a favor of us in an insolent manner making us unwilling to comply with his request. He did not mean to imply that we are to ask in this way.

G. Campbell Morgan, a great Congregational minister of yesteryear, commented on John 15:7: "When we abide in Christ and His words abide in us, we can literally demand what we will and it shall be granted." The word *demand* here needs some clarification.

Aiteo (or ask) can have the connotation of putting in a requisition. Picture a large supply depot with all kinds of items in storage. As part of the organization, you find yourself in need of a particular item in stock. You obtain a requisition slip, have it signed by the properly authorized person, and send it through channels. In a sense, your requisition is a "demand" in that it places a "demand" upon the existing supply. However, that "demand" or request is in no way arrogant or authoritarian. It is simply a request for supplies.

Here Jesus tells us that we can "requisition" from heaven's warehouse, knowing that when duly authorized by His signature (His name), our request will be honored and our need met. Let's ask largely and receive largely.

**. . your words have kept men on their feet,
the weak-kneed you have nerved.**

Job 4:4 Mof

Here Eliphaz is reminding his friend Job of how he has ministered to others in the past. In verse three Eliphaz remembers how Job . . . **set many right, and put strength into feeble souls** (*Mof*). Then in verse four he states that Job has given people words that have kept them on their feet.

This ability and capacity should be desired by all of us. In our speech, we can major on ministry. We can learn to use words that have a beneficial and supportive effect upon people. Our words can put people down or stand them up. Words can hurt or heal, blister or bless, destroy or deliver, tear down or build up. Job's words were so encouraging, they kept men on their feet and gave strength to the weak.

Some church groups and ministries which are now moving into prophecy (giving people words from the Lord) need to learn to put the emphasis on the positive promises of God. Before presuming to issue words of rebuke from the Lord, they first need to learn to speak forth His words of encouragement. The Lord tells us to edify or build people up. This does not refer to flattery, insincere praise, or "buttering up" people. It means giving people the words they need to keep them on their feet, determined to keep marching on to victory.

Make it a practice to speak wholesome, edifying, upbuilding words to friends, relatives, co-workers, and fellow Christians. Your words will keep many people on their feet in times of difficulty and will come back to you loaded down with many blessings. Start today!

**Don't let the world around you squeeze you into
its own mould, but let God re-make you . . . .**
Romans 12:2 Phillips

Part One

The ancient Greeks had two special words to describe
a thing or person. The words are *schema (skhay-mah)* and
morphe (mor-fay'). We can relate easily to these words because
of English derivations. *Schema* becomes scheme in English.
Morphe is recognized in the word *metamorphosis*, used to
describe the change of a larva into a butterfly or a polliwog
(tadpole) into a frog.

Schema has to do with externals — outward appearance,
shell, visible form or fashion, something molded into a
certain shape or fixture. The "scheme of things" thus refers
to the visible pattern of things.

Morphe has to do with internals — the inner nature of
a thing, situation, or person. In Christians, it points to their
character, integrity, and basic decency because of the
presence of the Christ-nature within them.

Schema can be transient and *morphe* can be quite
permanent. When Paul says in the *King James Version*,
**. . . be not conformed to this world: but be ye trans-
formed . . . .**, the first verb is derived from *schema*, the second
from *morphe*.

J.B. Phillips translates this verse with a touch of elegant
humor: **Don't let the world around you squeeze you into
its own mould, but let God re-make you . . . .** The whole
world system is transient, not permanent. It is unreal, since
God's kingdom is the only ultimate reality. According to this
word from the Lord, we do not need to lose a lot of sleep
worrying about how the world looks to us or at us!

Don't let the world around you squeeze you into its own mould, but let God re-make you . . . .
Romans 12:2 Phillips

Part Two

The *King James Version* says: . . . **be not conformed** (*schema*) **to this world: but be ye transformed** (*morphe*) **by the renewing of your mind** . . . . Renewal of the mind is an integral part and natural consequence of the New Birth.

One language expert has defined this transformation as "undergoing a complete change which, under the power of God, will find expression in character and conduct. *Morphe* lays stress on the inward change, while *schema* lays stress on the outward."

Today we are considered "real squares" if we don't keep up with current trends. Yet to truly "keep up" with all the latest and ever-changing fads, fashions, styles, and hit songs would require a 24-hour-a-day concentration.

Paul implies here that there is a certain amount of phoniness in the whole world system. He declares that conforming to the world's transient patterns is not for the Christian. Instead, the believer is to be transformed. To be transformed is to be "turned on to the Lord," lit up with His light, joy, glory, and honor. To be transformed is to unashamedly yet unpretentiously love the Lord with all one's heart, soul, mind, and strength. The transformed Christian is not overly concerned about the world's opinion of him because he knows that this world will soon pass away. Linked to eternity, he has been translated into a new dimension of living with a new priority list and a new value system. What a change!

"But that the world may know that I love the Father, and as the Father gave Me commandment, so do I. Arise, let us go from here."

John 14:31 NKJ

Jesus is our role model. The word *Christian* means "a diminutive Christ." It implies a person who thinks, acts, talks, serves, and speaks like Jesus. This verse shows us four outstanding qualities Jesus exhibited which can be strong motivation for us:

1. SACRIFICIAL LIFE: The very next day after this discourse, Jesus died on the cross. His words at this time all point to the fact that He came into the world for this one purpose — to give His life as a sacrifice for us so our sins could be forgiven us. The Righteous One gave Himself for the unrighteous. The Just died for the unjust.

2. LOVE: Jesus' death on the cross was motivated by love for mankind. In the crucifixion, God's love for man was demonstrated to the whole world.

3. OBEDIENCE: Jesus' earthly life was lived in perfect obedience to the divine will of the Father. The will of God dominated and determined His whole existence.

4. COURAGE: Jesus did all this with an unshaken courage: "Arise, let us go from here" is an expression of great bravery in the face of imminent death.

In 1825, Adam Clarke, a great commentator, stated: "All our actions should be formed on this example and plan. We should have the love of God and man for our principle and motive; God's glory for our end; His will for our rule. He who lives and acts thus shall live forever." This verse reveals a sacrificial nature, a motivating love, an obedient will, and an unflinching courage. May it describe us as well as it does our Lord.

"I will no longer talk much with you, for the ruler of this world is coming, and he has nothing in Me."

John 14:30 NKJ

Here the Lord Jesus is talking to His disciples about the enemy, Satan. **. . . he has nothing in Me,** He tells them. No power, no dominion, no mastery, no control, no handle, nothing to grasp on to — all these thoughts are expressed in this statement. Other translations of this phrase read: ". . . he has no hold over Me," ". . . he has no rights over Me," ". . . he has no sins to work on," ". . . he has no claims on Me," and . . . "he has nothing in common with Me."

It is as though the Lord is saying: "I am so completely covered by the Father's protection that there are no handles on Me for the enemy to grab hold of. Nothing about Me is available for his grasp."

The Lord has made it possible for all Christians to be completely covered by His righteousness and divine protection so that when the tempter comes to grapple with us, he can get no hold on us. The shield of faith is given to us to raise up against the fiery darts of the wicked one. This shield covers our total personality.

Every area of our life can be protected from Satanic assault. Our thoughts, words, imaginations, actions, will, work, recreation, social activities — all can be covered by the shield of faith. When Satan comes around to assail us, we will be able to say, "The ruler of this world is coming, but he has nothing in me. Nothing is exposed for his exploitation."

John says that the evil one cannot touch us. (1 John 5:18.) Praise God for His covering and protection.

> . . . **have mind of him wherever you may go, and he will clear the road for you.**
>
> **Proverbs 3:6 Mof**

Do you recall what automobile travel was like in the days before the development of modern highways? Most roads were narrow and winding as they followed the natural contour of the land. Traffic was slow and visibility limited. Motoring was dangerous and tiring. It seemed to take forever to get anywhere.

Now, by way of contrast, picture a modern interstate highway as it is laid out across the landscape. Today, rather than allowing the terrain to dictate the shape of the road, skilled engineers using heavy-duty equipment, huge earth-moving vehicles, and blasting powder, cut a wide, straight swath through every kind of natural obstacle and barrier. As a result, land travel has become so much easier, quicker, and safer. Due to carefully banked curves, graduated ascents, and increased visibility, traffic now glides safely and smoothly.

That is what this verse promises us. Bring the Lord into all your plans, and He will clear the road for you. Another version reads: ". . . he will direct your paths." *Direct* can mean "lead," "guide," or "show the way." It is also used as an adjective to indicate the shortest route between two points, as the most direct route from one city to another.

The Lord's guidance will always keep us from having to follow a round-about path. He will clear the road ahead of us and get us to our destination by the safest, straightest route possible. No back roads, no detours, no roadblocks, no lost time. Just straight ahead and on the right track!

> . . . I have been anointed with fresh oil.
> **Psalm 92:10** NKJ

Part One

In the Old Testament, kings, priests, and prophets were anointed with oil. Revelation 1:6 tells us that Jesus has made us believers kings and priests. We are also told that He has imparted prophecy to us. His three leadership functions have thus been transferred to us.

The Hebrew word translated **anointed** here is *balal (baw-lal')* and refers to mixing and mingling since the anointing oil was prepared by mixing together different ingredients.

In the nine gifts of the Holy Spirit (1 Cor. 12:8-10), three anointings can be seen:

The KINGLY anointing is evident in the word of wisdom, the word of knowledge, and the discerning of spirits. Proverbs 16:10 says: **Inspired decisions are on the lips of a king . . . .** (*RSV*).

The PRIESTLY anointing is evidenced in faith, miracles, and gifts of healing. Many times when Jesus healed the people, He sent them to the priests who were responsible for ministering to the sick and declaring them recovered.

The PROPHETIC anointing is represented by tongues, interpretation of tongues, and prophecy because these are vocal gifts.

Christians are anointed with the fresh oil of the Holy Spirit for kingly, priestly, and prophetic functions. All three anointings mingled together constitute the "fullness of God." (Eph. 3:19.) That fullness is ours for the asking.

. . . I have been anointed with fresh oil.
Psalm 92:10 NKJ

Part Two

A key word here is **fresh**. In Hebrew it is *ra'anan (rah-an-awn')* which is defined as: "flourishing, green, happy, cheerful, bright, new, luxuriant, prosperous." Besides indicating an anointing to set apart for service and to empower for spiritual ministry, this word embodies some additional features that can help us become better stewards of the Lord.

There is a refreshment implied in the word *ra'anan. The Bible In Basic English* translates this phrase, **. . . the best oil is flowing on my head,** while *The New International Version* renders it, **. . . fine oils have been poured upon me.** Moffatt's version reads, **. . . thou dost revive my failing strength.** All three indicate a before-and-after situation. Before anointing, we see a picture of a sun-baked desert traveler with dry skin, chapped lips, and languishing spirits. The anointing with fresh oil changes all that to a picture of vitality, exhilaration, and renewed vigor.

There is also an in-strengthening suggested here. One grammarian has defined *ra'anan* in these terse words: "The anointing in Psalm 92:10 seems also to imply a penetrating power." A fresh anointing can turn spiritual weariness into spiritual energy and revived strength.

Also in this word *ra'anan* is an association with hospitality, with the proper way an honored guest should be treated. (John 11:2; Luke 7:46; Psalm 23:5.) The compassionate Savior sees us journeying through the wilderness-world and bids us stop along our weary way to enjoy His hospitality, refreshment, and renewal.

. . . My elect shall long enjoy the work of their hands.
Isaiah 65:22 NKJ

Part One

One sector of the Christian Church has outlawed any kind of enjoyment. Their worship is icily cold. Their lifestyle is somber. Their conversation is solemn. Their daily existence is joyless. Such legalistic believers cannot smile because they do not have anything to smile about. By way of contrast, this verse promises an inward happiness of long duration.

It is sad that man's religion has taken the joy out of living. Some people cannot enjoy music, art, poetry, humor, possessions, or relationships. One lady feared enjoying her children too much lest the Lord should take them away. One man commented, "I just adore my wife and am greatly in love with her. Do you think Jesus will become jealous because I love my wife so much?" The answer came back, "No. Jesus would be jealous of His reputation for bringing happiness to a marriage if you did NOT love your wife."

Examine your heart and ask yourself the searching question: Am I able to enjoy my church? my family? my home? my work? my friends?

Satan wants to rob Christians of everything that could make for happiness in life. Our heavenly Father, because He loves us so dearly, wants us to enjoy life in all its fullness and abundance. (John 10:10.) His blessings upon us are expressions of His love for us. The way to enjoy all the good things the Lord gives us and does for us is simply to remember to keep Him in the center of our existence. When God is central, joy is universal.

. . . My elect shall long enjoy the work of their hands.
Isaiah 65:22 NKJ

Part Two

When I was preparing for the ministry, I was part of a religious group with a rigid caste system. A person's rank was reflected by the type of car he drove. The top executive leaders of the church drove luxury cars. People in a supervisory capacity drove top-of-the-line cars. Pastors with ten to twenty years seniority drove medium-sized cars. Those just starting out drove modest cars. Students fell into a category of wrecks, old bombs, junkers, and high-mileage used cars. This unofficial "pecking order" was not written anywhere in a manual, but eyebrows were raised if anyone dared to "get out of line." To do so was supposed to indicate pride — a deadly sin. To the hapless offender, the message was loud and clear: "Get back in your realm!"

On the very bottom rung of this organizational ladder, I as a Bible school student was put into a top-of-the-line luxury car by an interested friend. When I saw the negative reaction caused by my "impertinence" and "conceit," I purposed to sell the offending vehicle and settle for something more "becoming my low estate."

On my way down to automobile row, the Lord gave me this verse and this message: "I gave you this car to use and enjoy. Don't let man's opinion dictate to you or man's traditions dominate you. You will be doing a lot of driving. I want you to arrive at your destination safe and rested. Keep this car. Drive it. Enjoy it!"

I did just that. This verse became to me a promise of long-term duration. I had a good car plus a precious promise from a loving, caring, heavenly Father.

. . . **My elect shall long enjoy the work of their hands.**
Isaiah 65:22 NKJ

Part Three

The Hebrew word translated **long enjoy** is very unusual.
In the original text it is *balah (baw-law')* which is used 16 times
in the Old Testament. Except for this verse and Job 21:13,
balah always has to do with erosion, consuming, wearing
out, or wasting away.

Scholars are at a loss to reconcile long enjoyment with
a word used to describe the wearing down of life by the aging
process. When she heard the angel's message that she would
bear a son to Abraham in her old age, Sarah responded by
laughing in derision. In her reply to the message, she used
balah to describe herself: **After I have grown old** *(balah)* **shall
I have pleasure . . .?** (Gen. 18:12 NKJ). The answer was yes!

Bible words are so full of meaning and so rife with
possibilities. Fourteen times *balah* is used to indicate wear-
ing out through time. Twice it is used to refer to the utiliza-
tion of time for long-range benefit: ". . . My elect (the
followers of Christ) shall long enjoy the work of their hands.
Making full utilization of all the good things that go with
eternal life, My people shall last until time itself has come
to an end. Instead of wearing out, they will fully enjoy all
of Calvary's benefits and blessings."

Pleasures in the worldly scheme are short-lived.
Momentary thrills lead to a lifetime of remorse and regret.
Not so with the kingdom of God. Till the end of the age,
believers can see the work of their hands outlast and sur-
vive the fatigue and destruction that go with the passage
of time.

**Great peace have those who love Your law,
and nothing causes them to stumble.**

Psalm 119:165 NKJ

In the path of every forward-marching believer, there are booby traps, land mines, and obstacles. Satan's strategy is to keep us from reaching our appointed destination. In this verse, the psalmist assures us that by loving God's "law" we can get past all the hurdles, barriers, and stumbling blocks placed in our path. The filling of our hearts with the Word of God is the only sure way of overcoming the enemy's ambushes.

This **great peace** promised those who love and trust the Lord is so profound that with it in our hearts we can be assured of passing safely through all the danger zones that lie between us and our ultimate destination.

. . . nothing causes them to stumble. The psalmist also assures us that those who know and keep the commandments of the Lord will never stumble, falter, or fall by the wayside. Rooted and grounded in the will, the Word, and the love of God, they shall overcome.

Jesus said, **". . . blessed is he who is not offended because of Me"** (Luke 7:23 NKJ). If we are not ashamed of our Lord, if we are determined to trust and serve Him without doubting or complaining — even when we don't understand His dealings with us — then we can come through to victory regardless of circumstances.

Armed with this verse, you and I can daily overcome the sensual world, the carnal flesh, and the malignant devil. "Great peace without stumbling." What a word of assurance in a world full of tension, stress, and failure. Come what may, you and I can walk in confidence and *great* peace — 24 hours a day!

> . . . a man of understanding has a cool spirit.
>
> **Proverbs 17:27** AMP

In our day, the word "cool" has taken on a new significance. Among our youth, it is often considered the height of sophistication to be thought of as "cool." An individual who is "cool" is "street wise," "mod," "chic," "avant-garde," "hip." A "cool dude" is one who has "got it all together" — he's in total control of his own life and destiny. Everything about him is "cool, man, cool." He listens to "cool music," drives a "cool machine," is always seen in the company of "cool chicks."

Thus, the word *cool* is something of a "buzz word" to indicate those who are "on to something" or who "have something" that the rest of dull society is missing.

As far as we know, Solomon was the first man to use the word *cool* when he wrote: **. . . a man of understanding has a cool spirit.** Wise Solomon was not "trendy." His primary interest was not popularity or "peer group acceptance." He didn't follow fads or conform to the latest fashions — especially not in spiritual matters. Neither will a man (or woman) of understanding. The truly spiritual person is "cool" because he is disciplined and even-tempered. He doesn't "blow up," lose control, give vent to emotional outbursts, show temperament, or give in to moods.

In the original Hebrew, the word translated *cool* is *qar* (kar) and is defined as "quiet, calm, composed." The person with a "cool" spirit is self-possessed, free of anger, passion, or resentment. He is what every Christian should be. One writer has stated it well: "The ideal for all of us is to have a cool head and a warm heart." Let's be "cool" the Bible way!

> . . . he chose for himself five smooth
> stones from the brook . . . .
> ### 1 Samuel 17:40 NKJ

Why did David put five stones in his pouch when he only needed one to kill the giant?

Some scholars see a symbol of the five-fold ministry in this verse. (Eph. 4:11.) Others see a picture of the parable of the five wise virgins who had oil in their lamps and were ready for the arrival of the bridegroom. (Matt. 25:1-13.) Still others think the five stones represent the five books of Moses which make up the Jewish law. One scholar has suggested that the brook represents the Holy Spirit flowing continuously out of lives in love, power and wisdom.

Other experts hold that the five stones represent the law of God, or the Word of the Lord. The Word and the Spirit together provide the balance needed for victorious Christian living. Being full of the Word and Spirit of God is all that the believer needs to rid himself of the giants which would invade and conquer his personal Promised Land.

I would like to add another option to the list of possible meanings of the five stones. Some scholars believe that Goliath had four sons whom David ultimately faced and overcame. If the four sons mentioned in 2 Samuel 21:22 were the sons of Goliath, we can well understand why David chose five stones. His action was in preparation for overcoming the giant and his offspring. Instead of just barely getting by Goliath, David was ready for total and final victory.

God help us to use wisdom and foresight in all our planning. Amen!

. . . he who exalts his gate seeks destruction.
Proverbs 17:19 NKJ

Here is a call for modesty. It says to us: Don't build for arrogant ostentation, materialistic display, or as a demonstration of wealth.

The Hebrew word translated **gate** here is *pethach (peh-thak)* and is defined as "an opening, a doorway, or an entrance." In ancient times, for the purpose of utility and protection, people of modest means would build the entrance to their homes low to the ground, not more than three feet high. Thus marauders and thieves would not be able to ride their horses into the courts of the lower-income people to rob or attack them.

"Exalting the gate" (increasing the height and size of the entrance) was a symbol of increased affluence, prestige, and status. In contrast to the lower echelons, the wealthy would have high and wide gates to their estates so honored guests could ride on horseback or in carriages right up to the house. In a society composed of two economic extremes ("the haves" and "the have nots"), this architectural difference could easily incite ambition to become a "high-gater."

When invading Israel, Nebuchadnezzar honored the "low-gaters" by allowing them to choose whether they wanted to go away into captivity in Babylon or to remain in their homes. The "high-gaters" were given no such choice. They were carried away against their will and their homes burned to the ground. (2 Kings 25:9-12.)

Approximately 400 years earlier, Solomon might have foreseen all this and prophesied of it when he wrote that he who exalts his gate is asking for destruction. Some of us would be much better off staying low to the ground.

**Surely I have calmed and quieted my soul,
like a weaned child with his mother; like
a weaned child is my soul within me.**

Psalm 131:2 NKJ

This verse shows us how to progress from an attitude of getting things from the Lord to a desire to simply be near Him for the sheer pleasure of His presence. A weaned child takes nothing from his mother, yet he still seeks the comfort of being near her loving heart.

The Apostle Peter spoke of us as new-born babes. (1 Pet. 2:2.) He admonishes us to desire the sincere milk of the Word of God. The writer of Hebrews goes on to describe the difference between babes in Christ who feed on milk and those mature saints who feed on the solid food of the meat of the Word. (Heb. 5:12-14.)

The weaning process occurs when the child is no longer sufficiently nourished by the mother's milk. He is then given food that must be chewed. Mastication (chewing) is part of the growing up process and has spiritual significance.

The psalmist is saying to us here: "As a baby, I wanted to be close to my mother because she nursed me. As I grew, however, I learned to eat for myself. I still wanted to be close to my mother, but not for what she could provide for me materially.

"In the same way, as a spiritual baby I once sought the Lord for what He could give me. Now I seek Him for no other reason than to be close to Him, to be in His blessed presence. My happiness in the Lord is not dependent upon what He gives me or does for me; rather, my contentment comes from being near Him like a weaned child resting on his mother's comforting bosom."

". . .'He shall not come into this city, nor shoot
an arrow there . . . . By the way that he came,
by the same way shall he return . . . .'"
Isaiah 37:33,34 NKJ

This verse can be used to keep your thought life
undisturbed and in complete tranquility, serenity, and com-
posure.

Satan uses thoughts like flaming arrows to lodge in our
minds and arouse us to anxiety, fear, insecurity, anger, or
lust. The Greek word for *devil (diabolos)* is composed of two
words: *dia (dee-ah')*, "through," and *ballo (bal'-lo)*, "to throw."
Thus, it is Satan's strategy to attempt to "throw" (shoot)
arrows "through" (at) the believer to ignite trouble within
him. (Eph. 6:16.)

In this passage, the Lord is speaking through the pro-
phet Isaiah, telling the people of Israel that their enemy is
coming against them but that he will not be able so much
as to shoot an arrow into their city. As Christians, we can
have the same protection. Our minds can be so fortified with
the Word of God, our hearts so filled with His Spirit, our
walk of faith so undergirded with His divine presence and
support, that the enemy will have to flee the same way he
came against us.

Lately, I have been verbalizing a confession of faith to
contradict negative mental suggestions. I say: "That is not
my thought; I don't think that way. Lord, it's not Your
thought either, because it does not agree with Your written
Word." Then I quote a positive scripture in opposition to that
negative thought. Peace descends, and I can get on with
serving the Lord.

You can do the same. Resist the devil with the Word!

And Saul also went home to Gibeah; and valiant men went with him, whose hearts God had touched.

1 Samuel 10:26 NKJ

Here is a word about teamwork. It might be important to you, when planning your future, to consider the type of people with whom you will be working. In the Old Testament, God touched the hearts of valiant men and caused them to be willing to go with King Saul of Israel.

If you are obedient to His call upon your life, the Lord will move other people to want to assist you in accomplishing your God-given task. However, you must also do your part. Your gift will open the right doors for you, but it takes personal integrity and consistent character to continue to elicit support from others.

Our society fosters "Lone Rangers," superstars, and prima donnas. The Lord calls for teamwork and cooperation. Paul said it tersely in 1 Corinthians 3:6: one plants, another waters, and God gives the increase.

No one is a law unto himself. No one can finish the task alone. We need each other. Someone has said, "You are only as good as the people surrounding you." With this in mind, determine to: 1) be open to the teamwork concept, 2) expect quality people to want to join your team, 3) reject all concern about who will get the credit for a job well done, 4) concentrate on doing your best, and 5) work for God's glory and honor, not yours or someone else's.

Nothing else matters. As the Lord opens doors for you, look for the right people to work with you. Just as He has prepared you, so also He has prepared them. Together you make an unbeatable team — you, your "valiant men" (and women), and the Lord your God!

**"Because you would forget your misery, and
remember it as waters that have passed away."**
Job 11:16 NKJ

Here is a precious promise for us for the dislodging of
every unpleasant memory we retain.

There is an ocean called the Sea of God's Forgetfulness.
There is a river that washes away all our trangressions. There
is a fountain for sin and for uncleanness. (Zech. 13:1.)

All these images are given to us as a means of describ-
ing the current of cleansing water which washes away all
our past sins, mistakes, traumas, and defeats. The tide carries
them out and they are buried in the bottom of the ocean.

In Micah 7:19 (*NKJ*), the prophet says of his God:
. . . you will cast all our sins into the depths of the sea.
A famous evangelist of yesteryear stated, "When God cast
all our sins into the bottom of the ocean, He put up a sign
saying, 'No fishing allowed'!"

You and I can forget our past failures, past traumas, past
sins and mistakes. This verse assures us that they can be
put out of sight and out of mind. The Lord promises us here
to take the lid off our minds and to remove all the painful
residue from our past life. Good thoughts can then replace
miserable ones.

Serving the Lord offers us many benefits. Not the least
of these is a peaceful mind to replace a troubled one.

**. . . we should not trust in ourselves, but in
God who raises the dead, who delivered us
from so great a death, and does deliver us;
in whom we trust that He will still deliver us.**

2 Corinthians 1:10 NKJ

Here is a line from the past to the future: God has delivered us in the past, does deliver us in the present, and will deliver us in the future. This statement makes our confession of faith and our Christian witnessing simply a matter of declaring what the Lord has done, what He is doing, and what He is going to do.

Sometimes, fear suppresses our outward profession because we are hesitant to make any verbal pronouncement about the future. Uncertainty and insecurity tend to shut down our own interior faith and to quell our exterior Christian witness to others.

When some skeptic asks you, "How do you know God is going to heal you (or prosper you, or answer your prayer)?" how do you answer? Do you mouth vague expressions of wishful thinking? Do you make excuses for your own lack of firm assurance? *Do* you have any basis for expectation that God *will* intervene on your behalf?

Paul did. He would have answered that question like this: "I know that God is going to heal (prosper, answer) me because He has delivered me in the past and is delivering me in the present. Therefore, I am trusting Him to do the same in the future."

Since Jesus is the same yesterday, today, and forever (Heb. 13:8), and since our God has said, ". . . I am the Lord, I do not change . . ." (Mal. 3:6 NKJ), why not put your whole trust in Him for deliverance? Remember, Paul says that it is not ourselves that we trust, but God — the same Person Who delivered Christ (and us) from death.

Wherein I suffer trouble, as an evil doer, even unto bonds; but the word of God is not bound.

2 Timothy 2:9

The big word here is **bound**. In Greek it is *deo (deh'-o)*, a primitive verb root meaning "to chain, shackle, put in fetters, imprison."

Here Paul refers to his own prison confinement. He is suffering hardship and being treated like a common criminal. His ankles are in stocks and his wrists in irons. Yet joyfully he bursts forth with this praise report: "I am suffering imprisonment as though I were a criminal, but the Word of God is not bound."

Paul is telling us that although circumstances may try to limit, restrict, or bind us, we should always praise God that His promises can never be confined.

This verse reminds me of the story of the man who had gone grocery shopping for his family. On his way home, he was held up and robbed of all his food supplies. Still he came home brightly whistling a song of praise. His family couldn't understand how he could be so cheerful when he had just lost all their food. His reply was, "Oh, that man may have stolen our food, but we still have our appetite! He didn't get that!"

Paul could rejoice in the fact that even though he sat chained in a dark, dismal cell, the Word of God was out crisscrossing Asia Minor and turning people by the thousands to the Lord.

"I am limited in what I am able to do and where I can go," Paul admits. "But the promises of God know no limitations. He is still sending His Word and healing people everywhere!" (Ps. 107:20.)

. . . his commandments are not grievous.

1 John 5:3

When Jesus came to earth preaching the good news of God's love, the whole world was in a state of religious bondage. Even in Israel among God's own chosen people, the religious leaders of the day had imposed a harsh and burdensome legalistic code.

In Matthew 23:4 (*NKJ*), Jesus spoke to the multitudes about the scribes and Pharisees: **"For they bind heavy burdens, hard to bear, and lay them on men's shoulders; but they themselves will not move them with one of their fingers."** Our Lord was pointing out the tendency of religious people everywhere to impose upon others a dogmatic and tiresome system of doctrines, creeds, rituals, ceremonies, holy days, taboos, religious practices, formulas, confessions, and prescribed forms of worship and praise.

The Apostle John contrasts this kind of works program with what the Lord really desires: **"For this is the love of God, that we keep His commandments. And His commandments are not burdensome"** (1 John 5:3 *NKJ*). Another translation of this last phrase reads, ". . . His commandments are not irksome." Another renders it, ". . . His commandments are not hard to keep."

The Greek word translated **grievous** is *barus (bar-ooce')* which comes from a root word meaning "to overload." The Gospel liberates us from a rigid legalistic code of dos and don'ts. We find from experience that the Lord's yoke is easy and His burden light. Do you remember the heavy bondage you were in before your conversion to Christ? Now you are free!

**"For God so loved the world that He
gave His only begotten Son . . . ."**
John 3:16 NKJ

God so loved that He gave. Giving is the normal expression of love. When you love someone, you want to express that love by giving something of yourself.

Love prompts action. That action always originates from the lover and moves toward the person loved. In our case, it was God Who loved; we were the objects of that love which was expressed in Jesus Christ.

Our loving heavenly Father demonstrated His love for us, His creation, by giving His Son to redeem us when we had gone astray. By so doing, He ran the risk of having that love thwarted, misunderstood, and rejected. But God loved anyway, because love is His very nature.

Love not only gives, it gives the best. God gave His best when He gave His Son. This is another proof of God's love for us. Those who love want the one loved to have the very best.

Love not only gives the best, it gives it sacrificially. God revealed the unselfish nature of His love by freely sacrificing His own Son for our sakes.

Love not only gives the best, and sacrificially, it also gives generously and equally. God's love is so vast that each one of the 5 billion people on the earth today (as well as each of those who have ever lived or ever will live) is loved personally and individually by His Maker. God loves all of us completely and equally.

Because He loves, God gives. We, in turn, respond. Someone has said it succinctly: "Salvation is not an escape from the flames of hell, though those flames do exist. Salvation is a surrender to the love of God."

... **"Come aside by yourselves ...
and rest a while."** ...

Mark 6:31 NKJ

In Mark 6, we read how Jesus and the disciples could not function properly because the crowds kept coming and going, disrupting their normal eating and sleeping routines. Finally, the pressure of ministry became so great Jesus announced that it was time to draw aside and rest a while.

The key word here is **rest**. In the original Greek text, it is *anapauo (an-ap-ow-o)*. This word has three possibilities that speak to us today in our pressure-laden, stress-filled world:

Anapauo is the word used to describe an intermission in a play, an opera, a concert, or a stage production. This cessation is not only to give the audience a break in the action, but also so the artists and performers can have a moment to recuperate.

Anapauo also indicates recreation. This word can also be spelled re-creation. God created us originally, but from time to time we need to be physically, spiritually, mentally, and emotionally *re*-created. This can be accomplished through leisure-time activities such as fishing, camping, golfing, hiking, or picnicking — anything, in fact, that is totally different from our usual daily routine.

Anapauo also refers to refreshment. The Lord wanted the disciples to have a break in the action, to take some physical and spiritual refreshment, and then to go back to ministry with renewed strength and courage.

Anapauo. This could be a real word for us today: "Come aside by yourselves ... and rest a while. Then go back again rested, re-created, refreshed, and renewed."

August 29

. . . God wrought special miracles
by the hands of Paul.

Acts 19:11

A miracle is always special, so what does Luke mean here when he speaks of **special** miracles? Other versions of the Bible translate this word as "unusual," "extraordinary," or "uncommon." Since by definition a miracle is always something unusual, extraordinary, or uncommon, this verse is almost a play on words: "God wrought 'special specials,' 'extraordinary extraordinaries,' 'unusual unusuals' by the hands of Paul."

The thing that made these particular miracles so "special" was the geographic location in which Paul was ministering when they were performed. In New Testament days, the two cities most widely known for their total degeneracy and depravity were Corinth and Ephesus. Biblical scholars tell us that these two towns were open sewers of dissolution and debauchery. Yet they were the very areas God chose in which to perform the greatest miracles recorded in the book of Acts. Why?

There is a spiritual isometric that states, **. . . where sin abounded, grace did much more abound** (Rom. 5:20). Paul could well have been speaking of these two cities when he made that statement. The greater the sin, the greater the need of a Savior. The greater the presence of darkness, the greater the provision — and the power — of God's redeeming light.

That should encourage us today. Perhaps none of our modern-day cities compares in wickedness with Corinth and Ephesus, but God still has "special" miracles for each of them. Claim the "special" miracles of divine deliverance the Lord has for you and your hometown!

> " '. . . I will restore health to you and heal
> you of your wounds,' says the Lord, 'because
> they called you an outcast . . . .' "
>
> **Jeremiah 30:17** NKJ

There are definite compensations for patiently suffer-
ing resentment, rejection, and ridicule for the sake of the
Gospel and of Jesus Christ. (Matt. 5:11.) In my life, the
miraculous power and mighty presence of the Lord were
the most conspicuous when I stood alone in the midst of
persecution because of my Christian belief, lifestyle, and
witness.

In one place I worked, I found myself facing a constant
barrage of hostile, cutting words from antagonistic associates
who seemed to take delight in trying to discredit all Chris-
tians and Christianity in general. Since it was obvious that
I was a believer, these people made the most of every oppor-
tunity to "put me down." They did everything in their power
to make it appear that I was physically weak, intellectually
inferior, mentally deficient, emotionally unstable, and
socially unacceptable.

As painful as their constant harassment was, it did have
one positive result. In the midst of it, I became aware that
the Lord was doing a beautiful work of grace inside of me.
I realized that I was being sustained inwardly by a divine
power whose holy presence more than made up for what
I was suffering outwardly. (1 John 4:4.)

No one enjoys being an outcast. But it is encouraging
to remember that our patient endurance of shabby treatment
on the Lord's behalf kindles a positive response from Him
on our behalf that causes many good things to come our way!

> Teach me Your way, O Lord;
> . . . unite my heart to fear Your name.
>
> **Psalm 86:11** NKJ

Have you heard of the person who finally "got it all together," and then forgot where he put it?

In this verse, the psalmist prays for wisdom to know how to take all the different areas of his life and weave them together into a single strand of unity and strength. This passage has done a great deal to help me learn to bring my total being into harmony with itself, with the Holy Spirit, and with the rest of the Body of Christ.

In the original Hebrew text, the word translated **unite** in this verse is *yachad (yaw-khad')*. Grammarians define this word as "to join together, to become *one*." A genuine Christian is not a divided personality. Although comprised of different "parts," he is not really a "*triune* being"; rather, he is a *unified* being. His tangible and intangible bodies are inextricably interwoven together with each other and with the Spirit of His Maker. He is one with himself and His God.

The next step is to recognize that he is also one with his brothers and sisters in Christ. In such a fusion, there are no divisions, no separations, no barriers, no cross purposes, no conflicts of interest.

When believers truly become one Body, with Christ as Head, instead of going off in hundreds of different directions, we will finally be able to give total concentration to the one thing we are all called to do: worship the Lord and be witnesses to Him in all the world!

This verse is a good prayer, "Unite my heart to fear Your name."

References

New American Standard Bible (NAS). Copyright © 1960, 1962, 1963, 1968, 1971, 1972, 1973, 1975, 1977 by The Lockman Foundation, La Habra, California.

The Amplified Bible, New Testament (AMP). Copyright © 1954, 1958 by The Lockman Foundation, La Habra, California.

The Amplified Bible, Old Testament (AMP). Copyright © 1962, 1964 by Zondervan Publishing House, Grand Rapids, Michigan.

The Bible: A New Translation (Mof). Copyright © 1950, 1952, 1953, 1954 by James A.R. Moffatt, Harper & Row, Publishers, Inc., New York, New York.

The Holy Bible, New International Version (NIV). Copyright © 1973, 1978 by the New York International Bible Society. Used by permission of Zondervan Bible Publishers, Grand Rapids, Michigan.

The Holy Bible: Revised Standard Version (RSV). Copyright © 1946, 1952 by Division of Christian Education of the National Council of the Churches of Christ in the United States of America.

The Living Bible (TLB). Copyright © 1971 by Tyndale House Publishers, Wheaton, Illinois.

The Modern Language Bible, The New Berkeley Version In Modern English (MLB). Copyright © 1945, 1959 by Zondervan Publishing House, Grand Rapids, Michigan.

The New King James Version (NKJ). Copyright © 1984 by Thomas Nelson, Inc., Nashville, Tennessee.

The New Testament in Modern English (Phillips). Copyright © 1958, 1959, 1960, 1972 by MacMillian Publishing Co., Inc., New York, New York.

Dick Mills is intensely involved in the Scriptural renewal and personal upbuilding of the Body of Christ. He shares the "hidden riches of secret places" with sensitivity and compassion. Many have been touched by the hand of God through this man's dynamic ministry.

Pat Robertson, president of Christian Broadcasting Network, says: "Dick Mills has one of the most unique ministries of any man of God I know. God has gifted him with what amounts to a photographic memory containing thousands of scriptures. Under the anointing of the Holy Spirit and at an appropriate time, these words are brought forth to minister to the needs of individuals. Dick has been used of God to bring deep spiritual blessings at crucial times in my own life, and I'm sure this is true of tens of thousands of others around the country."

Dick and his wife Betty live in Hemet, California. This veteran of over thirty years has ministered to more than twenty denominations in countries throughout the world, including Israel, England, Australia, Singapore, Canada, and Latin America.

For a complete list of tapes and books
by Dick Mills, or to receive his
newsletter, *The Good Word Just For You*, write:

Dick Mills
P. O. Box 758
Hemet, CA 92343

*Please include your prayer requests and comments
when you write.*

**A Word In Season, Volumes I and II are
available from your local bookstore.**

Harrison House • P. O. Box 35035 • Tulsa, OK 74153

*Entries are arranged in the order that they appear in the book.